The Road through Romans

Strengthen Your Walk with Christ

Brenda Dillon

To David C. Egner, my former college professor and mentor.
Without his skillful editing and caring encouragement this
book would not be a reality.
Thank you, my friend.

Chapbook Press

Schuler Books
2660 28th Street SE
Grand Rapids, MI 49512
(616) 942-7330
www.schulerbooks.com

The Road Through Romans: Strengthen Your Walk with Christ

Copyright © 2022 by Brenda Dillon

ISBN 13: 9781957169262
Library of Congress Control Number: 2022919257

Cover by Bree Rose Creative LLC
Interior Design by Bree Rose Creative LLC

Printed in the United States by Chapbook Press

The Road through Romans

INTRODUCTION

The name "Christian" is often used as a label for someone who is thought to be a good person—having a personal relationship with the Lord Jesus Christ is not always a consideration. But in Paul's letter to the Believers in Rome, he is led by the Spirit of God to define true Christianity.

If we had only this letter to read, we would be fully informed about:

- Mankind's hopeless situation
- The great separation between God and man because of sin
- God's gracious plan for redeeming mankind through His Son
- Faith in Jesus is better than the Law and is for everyone
- The benefits of faith over the Law
- Life in Christ vs Life in the flesh
- The future blessings for every Believer
- Our security in Christ and His sovereignty
- The Israelites blew it but God WILL redeem them and keep His promises
- Our responsibilities to others as Believers in Jesus Christ
- Paul's example of the need for help and encouragement from others
- Paul's example of love for the Lord AND for the brethren

Paul systematically states Truth and goes on to explain it clearly so his readers can fully understand God's past, present, and future plan for the redemption of mankind.

The letter was most likely written around 57 A.D. In Romans 15:25-29 we read that Paul was on his way to deliver a gift offering to the impoverished Jewish Christians in Jerusalem—which we know he did on his third missionary journey.

He had not yet visited Rome and as you will see, sincerely looked forward to meeting with them. His desire, as with all the churches, was that they be firmly grounded in the good news/gospel of Jesus Christ and to continue to grow in their knowledge of God and His Son. He especially wanted his Jewish brethren to learn that trusting in Jesus was God's *new* way to be made right with Him. The Law—although good and true—could only point out their lost condition; it could not permanently change it. Only Faith in Jesus Christ could do that!!!

This Good News was for everyone—Jews and Gentiles alike. That means it's for you and me as well!

As we spend time together pondering over this special message and work of God, let it become our blueprint for living. Let it turn our complacency into urgency and our contentment with mediocrity into a challenge for excellence. Let it turn our hoarding of the Good News into seeking opportunities for sharing it with others.

We have a hope that is guaranteed—let's reach out to the hopeless and let God change their world.

Romans

DAY 1

1:1 - "This letter is from Paul, a slave of Christ Jesus, chosen by God to be an apostle and sent out to preach his Good News."

Paul, "a slave of Christ Jesus,"

Nearly ten years after Paul wrote this letter, the Apostle Peter described himself in the same way in his second letter to believers who had been scattered throughout the Roman Empire. To be a slave is to have one thing on your "to do" list—do what the master desires. You have one special person to please and be accountable to—the master. This is how the Apostles saw their calling by Jesus. However, it was not a forced position of enslavement, it was a chosen commitment—not only to the One who called them, but it extended to the fulfillment of Jesus' work of building His kingdom.

These men had spent time with their Master. They had learned to love and trust Him. We have that same privilege. As we read His word and talk it over with Him, His Holy Spirit, living within us, draws our attention to the truth He wants us to know and understand. Whether it's a special promise He wants to bless us with, a specific sin He wants us to repent of, a previously unknown insight into Him, a warning, a job He has for us, or an answer we've been seeking—He is at hand! We can trust Him. We can be sure of His presence every moment of every day. He wants to use us. He wants us on board with spreading His Good News.

CHALLENGE: Have you, like Paul, chosen to be a slave of Jesus? Are *His* desires at the top of your list of priorities? Does your heart desire to be involved in His kingdom work?

*After examining your heart in prayer, write down any insights or steps the Lord may give you to help deepen your commitment to Christ and your involvement in His eternal work.

9

DAY 2

1:2-4 – "God promised this Good News long ago through his prophets in the holy Scriptures. The Good News is about his Son. In his earthly life he was born into King David's family line, and he was shown to be the Son of God when he was raised from the dead by the power of the Holy Spirit. He is Jesus Christ our Lord."

The "Good News" should not have been new news to the Jews.

The prophets in the Old Testament were given messages concerning the Son of God. Isaiah 7:14 foretells His virgin birth. Micah 5:2 says He would be born in Bethlehem from the clans of Judah. Zechariah 9:9 predicts His ride into Jerusalem on a donkey and King David wrote a song about His pierced hands and feet, and the dividing of His garments. (Ps. 22:16-18)

When Isaiah was given the message we read in the fifty third chapter of his book his heart must have been heavy indeed. However, Isaiah was also the prophet to proclaim, "He will swallow up death forever!" Job declared, "But as for me, I know that my Redeemer lives and He will stand upon the earth at last." (Isaiah 25:8, Job 19:25)

Paul wants his readers to know that this Good News, promised by God through the prophets, was fulfilled in His Son, Jesus Christ. His Jewish readers would have been well versed in what the Scriptures said about the coming Messiah; but to their Gentile brethren, this was breaking news.

The saints of old *looked ahead* with anticipation for God's redemption plan to be fulfilled. Future generations would be able to *look back* in humble gratitude at the redemptive work of Jesus Christ. For both Jew and Gentile, the common bond would be the hope of eternal life in Christ.

CHALLENGE: Read I Peter 1:10-12 and imagine being one of the Old Testament prophets who received the message that a Messiah would one day come, bringing salvation to all who believed in His name. Now imagine how you would feel if you were told that the message was not for you but for future generations.

READ: Genesis 15:6, Hebrews 11:4, and Romans 4:1-3 and record how these Old Testament saints were saved—made right with God. What did God see in their hearts?

DAY 3

1:5-7 – "Through Christ, God has given us the privilege and authority as apostles to tell Gentiles everywhere what God has done for them, so that they will believe and obey him, bringing glory to his name. And you are included among those Gentiles who have been called to belong to Jesus Christ. I am writing to all of you in Rome who are loved by God and are called to be his own holy people. May God our Father and the Lord Jesus Christ give you grace and peace."

Paul was not your average, everyday Jew.

Paul was a full-fledged, well-trained Pharisee. He knew the Scriptures taught that a Jewish Messiah would come to save His people and set up His kingdom. Not until after his experience with the resurrected Messiah did he learn this salvation would be offered to ALL people—Jew and Gentile alike. His honor would be to spread the Good News to the Gentiles, who would be loved by God and called to be His holy people. Paul would do so with the same fervor he had persecuted Jesus' followers.

As people began to believe in Jesus Christ, Paul's heart was full of joy because he knew this was pleasing God—*which was his reason for serving Him.* (I Thess. 2:4)

CHALLENGE: We must ask ourselves, do we serve Jesus with this same desire as our motivator, or are we willing to settle for the "praise of man" in the here and now? How eager are we to serve God?

READ: Jonah 1:1-2 and Jonah 3:10-4:3 - How eager was Jonah to serve God? What do you think was motivating Jonah?

READ: Jonah 4:11. What was motivating God in His assignment for Jonah?

11

DAY 4

1:8-15 –"Let me say first that I thank my God through Jesus Christ for all of you, because your faith in him is being talked about all over the world. God knows how often I pray for you. Day and night I bring you and your needs in prayer to God, who I serve with all my heart by spreading the Good News about his Son. One of the things I always pray for is the opportunity, God willing, to come at last to see you. For I long to visit you so I can bring you some spiritual gift that will help you grow strong in the Lord. When we get together, I want to encourage you in your faith, but I also want to be encouraged by yours. I want you to know, dear brothers and sisters, that I planned many times to visit you, but I was prevented until now. I want to work among you and see spiritual fruit, just as I have seen among other Gentiles. For I have a great sense of obligation to people in both the civilized world and the rest of the world, to the educated and uneducated alike. So I am eager to come to you in Rome, too, to preach the Good News."

The Good News was also *big news* to the world.

His message may have been new news to the Gentiles but as they began to trust in Jesus Christ as their savior, their new found faith became the talk of the town.

We are not certain how the church in Rome was started—perhaps with the growing population of Jewish converts living there—it was a gathering of both Jewish and Gentile believers. Paul had not yet met with them but desperately wanted to do so. Perhaps his recent letters to the Corinthian church and his need for addressing their sinful compromising and confusing practices was motivating his need to encourage the believers in Rome and to be encouraged by them in return.

He prayed diligently for their spiritual growth and held firmly to his God-given responsibility of spreading the gospel of Jesus Christ. His love for his master gave him a sense of obligation that drove him until the day he died. He never quit! He finished the job God had given him to do. (II Timothy 4:6-8)

CHALLENGE: It's easy to give up and hard to keep going—especially when faced with opposition or struggles. But when we keep going, there is victory!

READ: Acts 19:20, 17:6, and 24:5 - Describe the effect of Paul's preaching. How far did it reach and was it well accepted? Explain your answer.

DAY 5

1:16-17 – "For I am not ashamed of this Good News about Christ. It is the power of God at work, saving everyone who believes—the Jew first and also the Gentile. This Good News tells us how God makes us right in his sight. This is accomplished from start to finish by faith. As the Scriptures say, 'It is through faith that a righteous person has life.'"

We must believe the bad news before we will embrace the Good News.

Paul was not ashamed of the Good News. Why? Because he understood and believed the bad news. That is, all have sinned—all fall short of God's holy standard. No one has the ability to be as righteous as God. Paul even says he's the worst sinner of all. (I Tim. 1:15) But Paul also believed the Good News—Jesus died for our sins and was raised from the dead on the third day by the power of God, according to the scriptures. (I Cor. 15:3-4)

When we believe the Good News and by faith trust Jesus Christ to be our Redeemer, the same power that raised Jesus from the dead makes us right with God. Paul was not ashamed or embarrassed of being connected with Christ because he knew and believed that HE was the source of his life—both physical and spiritual. He knew that his only hope of being forgiven of his sin and being made right with God rested in the Good News of Jesus Christ. And Paul boldly testified of it wherever he went.

CHALLENGE: Paul was not ashamed of Christ and His Good News, he willingly suffered persecution and prison for the sake of His name. This kind of devotion is a wonderful example and testimony to us.

READ: Luke 9:26 – How important is it to God that we not be ashamed of Jesus and the Good News about Him? Explain your answer.

READ: II Timothy 1:8 – What does Paul tell Timothy to be ready to do?

13

DAY 6

1:18-20 – "But God shows his anger from heaven against all sinful, wicked people who suppress the truth by their wickedness. They know the truth about God because he has made it obvious to them. For ever since the world was created, people have seen the earth and sky. Through everything God made, they can clearly see his invisible qualities—his eternal power and divine nature. So they have no excuse for not knowing God."

God cannot be hidden. His truth will be revealed.

Mankind has always tried to ignore God and the truth of His existence. Driven by the sin nature, we do our best to manufacture ways of bypassing Him or ignoring His presence altogether. However, Jesus told the Pharisees, if his people stopped praising Him and His mighty works, the rocks on the ground would cry out in praises. (Luke. 19:40)

He has made Himself known to man—HE IS NOT A SECRET!!!

The heavens proclaim His existence day after day—night after night. His power and divine personality can be seen throughout His creation. (Ps.19:1-4) All mankind has access to Him and to the truth about Him. Sadly, few pursue Him.

CHALLENGE: Take time to recognize God's presence. He wants us to know Him. He wants us to love and need Him. He wants us to live like we believe He is HERE! Start recording every time you see the hand of God at work. Review your notes often and it will surprise you how busy God is in your life and in the world around you.

READ: II Peter 3:3-6 - What important events are spoken of here that wicked people deliberately like to forget? Why would the enemy want these events erased from the minds of mankind? What affect could it have on the prophetic words in the Scriptures?

DAY 7

1:21-22 – "Yes, they knew God, but they wouldn't worship him as God or even give him thanks. And they began to think up foolish ideas of what God was like. As a result, their minds became dark and confused. Claiming to be wise, they instead became utter fools."

Is there a difference between knowledge and wisdom???

I like to think of knowledge as a gigantic book containing all the information mankind is ever able to know or learn. Wisdom is knowing what to do with it. However, this leads us to another dilemma. Knowing what to do with what we've learned is still useless if we have no ability or power for *choosing* to act on it. This is where the indwelling Spirit of Jesus Christ comes in. *His* light and life allows us to see truth, understand it, and then *choose* to live it by the power of the Holy Spirit.

The people described in these verses knew God but they *chose* not to worship or love Him. Therefore, they had no capacity for seeing or understanding truth. They were utter fools for refusing to worship or give thanks to God—the only One worthy of praise.

Choosing to have Jesus Christ in our heart gives us *His* life and power to live out the wisdom and truth He teaches us. Our worship of Him becomes our joy and privilege—not just our duty.

CHALLENGE: When we give God His rightful place as Creator, Lord, Savior, and Abba Father, our natural response will be a desire to worship and praise Him. This oneness opens the door to wisdom and understanding through His Spirit.

READ: Proverbs 2:6, Colossians 2:3, and James 1:5 - How do we get wisdom, knowledge, and understanding?

READ: Ephesians 1:16-17 and record what Paul prayed for on behalf of the brethren in Ephesus.

15

DAY 8

1:23-28 – "And instead of worshiping the glorious, ever-living God, they worshiped idols made to look like mere people and birds and animals and reptiles. So God abandoned them to do whatever shameful things their hearts desired. As a result, they did vile and degrading things with each other's bodies. They traded the truth about God for a lie. So they worshiped and served the things God created instead of the Creator himself, who is worthy of eternal praise! Amen. That is why God abandoned them to their shameful desires. Even the women turned against the natural way to have sex and instead indulged in sex with each other. And the men, instead of having normal sexual relations with women, burned with lust for each other. Men did shameful things with other men, and as a result of this sin, they suffered within themselves the penalty they deserved. Since they thought it foolish to acknowledge God, he abandoned them to their foolish thinking and let them do things that should never be done."

"...so God abandoned them..."

What could possibly be worse?! What would provoke God to leave us?

If we examine these verses closely, we see THE cause for this godly abandonment.

Verse 23 – Instead of worshiping God, they worshiped idols.

Verse 25 – They traded the truth about God for a lie and worshiped the creation instead of the Creator who is worthy of praise.

Verse 28 – They thought it foolish to acknowledge God.

SO......

Verse 24 – God abandoned them.

Verse 26 – That is why God abandoned them.

Verse 28 – He abandoned them.

As a result of their refusal to worship God, He abandoned them. They were released from all moral restraint. They were given free rein to do every shameful, vile thing their dark minds could imagine, and they *suffered within themselves.*

Looking elsewhere for peace, joy, forgiveness, and fulfillment has left this world in a state of despair—emptiness, frustration, striving, boredom, and

16

loneliness leads to an onslaught of broken lives, broken families, suicide, and substance abuse. In Isaiah 45:22 God says, "Let all the world look to me for salvation! For I am God; *there is no other.*"

As followers of Jesus Christ, we know the truth!!! We need to let others know God is real—He is sovereign—He **is** the answer—He can be trusted—*He **alone** is worthy of our worship*!

"Since we are receiving a Kingdom that is unshakable, let us be thankful and please God *by worshiping Him* with holy fear and awe." (Hebrews 12:28) (Italics added)

CHALLENGE: Psalm 29:1-2, 10. Only God is worthy of our worship and praise.

READ: Deut. 32:16 and Exodus 34:14 - Explain what made God angry and why?

17

DAY 9

1:29-32 – "Their lives became full of every kind of wickedness, sin, greed, hate, envy, murder, quarreling, deception, malicious behavior, and gossip. They are backstabbers, haters of God, insolent, proud, and boastful. They invent new ways of sinning, and they disobey their parents. They refuse to understand, break their promises, are heartless, and have no mercy. They know God's justice requires that those who do these things deserve to die, yet they do them anyway. Worse yet, they encourage others to do them, too."

Only God has the ability to keep one from falling away. (Jude 24)

Refusing to acknowledge God results in spiritual abandonment from His protection and guidance and a downward spiral into unrighteousness—described here in verses 29-31.

Follow it down…

Being released from God allows the sinful nature to suppress the law of God that has been planted in the heart of mankind—killing the conscience to the point of not caring what is right or wrong—allowing the sinful nature to then take total control; naturally desiring more of what the world offers. This can lead to hatred and jealousy of those who "have it all"—going so far to be willing to kill to get it. Arguments are made to justify wicked behavior; using deception to manipulate and malign to gain power, position, or popularity. Hatred of God, who would disapprove of this evil behavior, brings about a self-appointed position and an arrogant attitude of superiority. Having the ability to dream up evil ways that are always growing worse, there is no ability or desire for understanding—even when coming from parents. There is no trust, no softness in the heart, no love, no concern outside of self.

As Christians, we have God's Holy Spirit within us—our *guarantee that He will never leave us*. However, until we die, we also possess our sinful human nature that is at war with God. (Paul fully understood this battle within and described it later in chapter seven) But we are still susceptible to sin. Worldliness can make us callous to God's righteous moral values—the very thing that guides our behavior.

CHALLENGE: We *must* make every effort to stay closely connected in our relationship with Christ and to be learning His Word.

READ: Psalm 119:11, Psalm 1:1-2, and Galatians 5:16 - How does God say we can keep from falling away from Him?

18

Romans 2:1-4 – "You may think you can condemn such people, but you are just as bad, and you have no excuse! When you say they are wicked and should be punished, you are condemning yourself for you who judge others do these very same things. And we know that God, in his justice, will punish anyone who does such things. Since you judge others for doing these things, why do you think you can avoid God's judgment when you do the same things? Don't you see how wonderfully kind, tolerant, and patient God is with you? Does this mean nothing to you? Can't you see that his kindness is intended to turn you from your sin?"

"What goes around comes around."

When we point fingers at others, eventually they come back to us. Not one of us is exempt from sin. Ours may be different from our neighbors, but ALL sin is worthy of God's righteous judgment. Focusing on the sins of others takes our eyes off God and our own need for His loving scrutiny. (Psalm 139:23-24)

God wants us to recognize OUR sin, and His patience gives us the opportunity to repent of it. Peter said His patience also gives people time to be saved. (II Peter 3:9) This is God's grace and mercy working together!

CHALLENGE: We must not take God's patience for granted by testing Him. Take advantage of His patience with a timely repentant heart that brings us back into a close relationship with Jesus.

READ: II Corinthians 7:10-11 - What can lead to repentance and even to salvation? Now read James 2:13 and record what triumphs over judgment. If our heart is filled with mercy toward others, what will we not be inclined to do?

DAY 11

2:5-11 – "But because you are stubborn and refuse to turn from your sin, you are storing up terrible punishment for yourself. For a day of anger is coming, when God's righteous judgment will be revealed. He will judge everyone according to what they have done. He will give eternal life to those who keep on doing good, seeking after the glory and honor and immortality that God offers. But he will pour out his anger and wrath on those who live for themselves, who refuse to obey the truth and instead live lives of wickedness. There will be trouble and calamity for everyone who keeps on doing what is evil—for the Jew first and also for the Gentile. But there will be glory and honor and peace from God for all who do good—for the Jew first and also for the Gentile. For God does not show favoritism."

Because YOU are stubborn. Because YOU refuse His righteous standards.....

This is mankind's free-will hitting head-on with God's sovereign righteousness. God says, "You must...", we say, "We won't...". If this condition is not rectified, we will experience the consequences described here as *God's righteous judgment.*

Each of us has the freedom and ability to choose to say no to God and live the way *we* think is best, or say yes to Him and live in obedience to His word. However, God will use *our own choices* to either reward us with glory, honor, peace, and eternal life for choosing to follow Him, or we condemn ourselves with wrath, indignation, affliction, distress, and eternal separation from God if we choose to reject Him. We cannot expect God's help, blessing, and deliverance if we have made the decision to shut Him out of our life. The choice is ours to make, and it will be one way or the other—there's no in between.

CHALLENGE: Choosing to follow Jesus and allowing Him to have authority in our lives, gives us access to His salvation, power and blessing. For apart from Him, we can do nothing. (John 15:5)

READ: John 3:36 - What are the two choices given in this verse and the end result of each one?

READ: II Corinthians 5:10 - Is there any doubt that ALL of us will stand before God? When we do, what will be judged?

READ: II Corinthians 5:15 - Again, what two choices are repeated here and how do we know that everyone has the same opportunity for choosing eternal life?

20

2:12-16 – "When the Gentiles sin, they will be destroyed, even though they never had God's written law. And the Jews, who do have God's law, will be judged by that law when they fail to obey it. For merely listening to the law doesn't make us right with God. It is obeying the law that makes us right in his sight. Even Gentiles, who do not have God's written law, show that they know his law when they instinctively obey it, even without having heard it. They demonstrate that God's law is written in their hearts, for their own conscience and thoughts either accuse them or tell them they are doing right. And this is the message I proclaim—that the day is coming when God, through Christ Jesus, will judge everyone's secret life."

No one has an excuse. No one gets a free ticket.

The best way to explain this passage is by breaking it down like this:

Creation: Adam and Eve were created in God's image. Their human nature knew only *light*—God's *right*eous standard. They were ignorant and innocent of sin and wrong.

The Fall: Their eyes were opened to sin. (Gen. 3:22) Their human nature was no longer ignorant or innocent of wrong but guilty of sin. Right and wrong were both known and at war within the heart of man.

The Law: This was given to the nation of Israel to spell out God's righteous standard. It was obeyed by some and manipulated by others to fit human standards. The war between right and wrong continued. Even the Gentiles, who didn't have the written Law, had light within them that battled with darkness. Right vs wrong.

The Good News: Jesus Christ offers salvation for all who by faith receive Him. His Holy Spirit comes to dwell within their heart, to illuminate God's righteousness and give them *His* power to *live in His righteousness*.

However, mankind will still be held accountable for their *response* to what has been revealed to them. Some may *know* plenty but refuse to obey or accept it. Others may *know* little but choose to obey it and take it to heart. All mankind will be judged on the basis of what is in their heart, not on what is in their head.

CHALLENGE: If we know the Scriptures but don't live according to them, our knowledge is of no benefit to us or God.

READ: James 4:17 and Luke 12:48 - Explain these verses.

DAY 13

2:17:24 – "You who call yourselves Jews are relying on God's law, and you boast about your special relationship with him. You know what he wants; you know what is right because you have been taught his law. You are convinced that you are a guide for the blind and a light for people who are lost in darkness. You think you can instruct the ignorant and teach children the ways of God. For you are certain that God's law gives you complete knowledge and truth. Well then, if you teach others, why don't you teach yourself? You tell others not to steal, but do you steal? You say it is wrong to commit adultery, but do you commit adultery? You condemn idolatry, but do you use items stolen from pagan temples? You are so proud of knowing the law, but you dishonor God by breaking it. No wonder the Scriptures say, "The Gentiles blaspheme the name of God because of you.'"

Do as I say, not as I do!

This philosophy doesn't get anyone very far, but the Jewish leaders were masters of it. They could spout the Law and wag their fingers at others, but Jesus called them "whitewashed tombs"—beautiful on the outside, but filled with hypocrisy and lawlessness on the inside. It's no wonder those looking on were disgusted by their teachings.

To be effective in God's kingdom work we must wear His name well from the inside out. Our hearts need to be so in tune with God that *He* flows from us. It will be *His* beauty that draws people to His truth. We have the honor and privilege of serving as the "bait." Will we be real bait—able to feed and nourish—or will we be fake bait, like the Pharisees, leaving an offensive taste in the mouth?

"Jesus called out to them, "Come, follow me, and I will show you how to fish for people!'" (Matthew 4:19)

CHALLENGE: If we are to represent Jesus Christ in this world, we must look and act like Him. Others must be able to see His character and His heart in us.

READ: I Timothy 4:16 and I Peter 3:15 - These verses give us instruction on how our life and words can affect the life of others. Explain how this can lead to someone's salvation.

2:25-29 – "The Jewish ceremony of circumcision has value only if you obey God's law. But if you don't obey God's law, you are no better off than an uncircumcised Gentile. And if the Gentiles obey God's law, won't God declare them to be his own people? In fact, uncircumcised Gentiles who keep God's law will condemn you Jews who are circumcised and possess God's law but don't obey it. For you are not a true Jew just because you were born of Jewish parents or because you have gone through the ceremony of circumcision. No, a true Jew is one whose heart is right with God. And true circumcision is not merely obeying the letter of the law; rather, it is a change of heart produced by God's Spirit. And a person with a changed heart seeks praise from God, not from people."

There is no coattail riding allowed!!

Some in the Jewish community were claiming religious superiority by virtue of their heritage and the ceremony of circumcision—both being *outward* evidence. But Paul wanted them to take a look at the *inward* evidence—is their heart in obedience to the law? This is the evidence God looks at. (I Samuel 16:7)

To God, an uncircumcised Gentile whose heart was in obedience to Him through the work of His Spirit was more honorable than a circumcised Jew whose heart was disobedient to His law.

No matter how good we look on the outside, it's what's on the inside that sets us apart to God. Our religious heritage or hard work cannot make us right with Him. We must choose to trust Jesus Christ for that. Then His Holy Spirit can begin to change us from the inside out—giving *God* cause for praise!

CHALLENGE: Salvation cannot be handed down through ancestral blood. It can only be gained through the blood of Jesus Christ.

READ: I Peter 1:2, Hebrews 9:14, and Psalm 51:10 - These verses speak of being cleansed. Record *who* does the cleaning, *what* does the cleansing, and what is the result of being cleansed.

23

DAY 15

3:1-3 – Then what's the advantage of being a Jew? Is there any value in the ceremony of circumcision? Yes, there are great benefits! First of all, the Jews were entrusted with the whole revelation of God. True, some of them were unfaithful; but just because they were unfaithful; does that mean God will be unfaithful?"

Abandon His people??? When pigs fly!!

What advantage is there in being a Jew? Why were they His special people?

God chose to have His Son's earthly heritage rooted in the nation of Israel. He chose the Jewish nation to be Jesus' family and ancestors. Even when they rejected God and ultimately rejected and killed His Son, they remained His chosen people. He remained—and still remains—faithful to them.

It was to the Jewish nation that God chose to reveal His code of righteousness when He gave them the Ten Commandments and the Law. Their obedience and commitment to their God and His holy standard set them apart in a world full of sin and godlessness. Even in their times of rebellion against Him, God held tight to His covenant with them. In Jeremiah 31:36-37, God says He would sooner do away with all natural laws—making the universe able to be measured and the earth's foundation able to be explored—before He would break His covenant with His people.

As children of His new covenant—joint heirs with Jesus; a people saved by faith in the blood of Jesus Christ—we have the same promise of His faithfulness. He will NEVER leave us or abandon us. (Hebrews 13:5)

CHALLENGE: John 10:29 says, "no one can snatch us from the Father's hand." We are securely held in an eternal grip motivated by love and grace.

READ: Psalm 94:14 - How does this verse refer to us His people?

READ: II Timothy 2:13 - Explain this verse.

READ: Ephesians 1:14 – What special guarantee did God give us and what does it promise?

3:4 – "Of Course not? Even if everyone else is a liar, God is true. As the Scriptures say about Him, 'You will be proved right in what you say, and you will win your case in court.'"

Until a person agrees with God's "Guilty of sin" verdict, they cannot be saved.

Claiming to be innocent doesn't make one innocent—the judge will still render his decision based on the truth. And because the Judge is the Creator of truth, His judgment will always be just and fair.

Paul defends God's righteousness by quoting from Psalm 51:4. David had been confronted by the prophet Nathan with his sin of adultery and murder. He recognized it, agreed with God's guilty verdict, and surrendered with a repentant heart to God's authority and judgment. He brought his heart back into line with God's heart.

Because of God's holy and righteous character, He can be trusted to ALWAYS judge fairly—good news for the innocent, bad news for the guilty offender. (I Peter 2:23) Also in keeping with His character, He will ALWAYS forgive a repentant heart. His desire is to hold us close to Himself. We're the ones who drift away. Once again we can use David as an example. His prayer was, "Search me, O God, and know my heart; test me and know my anxious thoughts. Point out anything in me that offends you, and lead me along the path of everlasting life." (Ps. 139:23-24)

CHALLENGE: David repented immediately after recognizing his sin. He didn't debate it, try to justify it, or slough it off. We must follow his example and come back quickly into the forgiving arms of God.

READ: Job 22:21 – What comes with repentance?

READ: Psalm 50:6 – What here is proclaimed and what will God be?

READ: Acts 15:7 – How does God look at our repentance?

DAY 17

3:5-8 – "But," some might say, 'Our sinfulness serves a good purpose, for it helps people see how righteous God is. Isn't it unfair, then, for him to punish us?' (This is merely a human point of view.) Of course not! If God were not entirely fair, how would he be qualified to judge the world? 'But,' someone might still argue, 'How can God condemn me as a sinner if my dishonesty highlights his truthfulness and brings him more glory?' And some people even slander us by claiming that we say, 'The more we sin, the better it is!' Those who say such things deserve to be condemned.'"

How can God judge us for our sin if our sin turns the spotlight on His righteousness?

This is not as hard as it may seem. Simply said, God knows every heart. If our motive is to honor God and be a reflection of His righteousness, He knows it—for "He alone examines the motives of our hearts." (I Thessalonians 2:4) However, if we attempt to excuse or justify our sin on the pretense of exposing God's righteousness, He knows that as well. God gave this message to Jeremiah the Prophet, "... I, the Lord, search all hearts and examine secret motives. I give all people their due rewards, according to what their actions deserve." (Jeremiah 17:10)

As an example—how foolish would it be for a group of students to make a pact to fail all their classes so that another student would be assured of winning the "Highest Honors" award? They would be sealing their own fate to make the other student *look good*. No one wins!

CHALLENGE: We bring attention to God's goodness by *imitating* it, not by attempting to contrast it. He knows the difference because He alone knows the thoughts and intentions of the heart.

READ: Matthew 5:16 – What does this verse say brings praise to our heavenly Father?

READ: Ephesians 5:1 and John 14:12 – Why are we to imitate God? If we are true believers what will we do?

DAY 18

3:9-12 – "Well then, should we conclude that we Jews are better than others? No, not at all, for we have already shown that all people, whether Jews or Gentiles, are under the power of sin. As the Scriptures say, 'No one is righteous—not even one. No one is truly wise; no one is seeking God. All have turned away; all have become useless. No one does good, not a single one.'"

Without having the life of Jesus Christ living within us, everything we do, say, think, desire, hope for, put our trust in is motivated by "self"—sin.

Even though the Jews were God's chosen people they were still sinners in need of a savior. Every human being born in sin has a natural desire for things that are contrary to God's character. The Scriptures say, "When Adam sinned, sin entered the world. Adam's sin brought death, so death spread to everyone, for everyone sinned." (Romans 5:12)

This puts us in a hopeless position.

Being enslaved by sin keeps our minds darkened to truth and wisdom. Without God's prompting, we would never be able to see Him or seek Him. Our will would always be at odds with His. Without Jesus' life in us there would be no spiritual fruit, for it is His indwelling presence that empowers and motivates us to love, to do good, to be patient and kind, to be faithful and gentle, to have self-control. His Holy Spirit offers us inner peace and joy that can overpower anything this world throws at us. The bottom line is this:

Without Him we can do nothing. (John 15:5)

Through Him we can do all things. (Philippians 4:13)

CHALLENGE: We must *seek* God. It must be a conscious decision to grow in our knowledge of Him and to allow Him to have control of our heart and life every day. Isaiah 55:6

READ: I Corinthians 2:14 – What is needed for us to have the ability to understand spiritual things? Without it, how do spiritual things appear?

READ: Psalm 10:4 – What keeps mankind from seeking God?

READ: Jeremiah 29:13 – What happens when we seek God with our whole heart?

What does Isaiah 55:6 challenge us to do?

27

DAY 19

3:13-20 – "Their talk is foul, like the stench from an open grave. Their tongues are filled with lies. Snake venom drips from their lips. Their mouths are full of cursing and bitterness. They rush to commit murder. Destruction and misery always follow them. They don't know where to find peace. They have no fear of God at all. Obviously, the law applies to those to whom it was given, for its purpose is to keep people from having excuses, and to show that the entire world is guilty before God. For no one can ever be made right with God by doing what the law commands. The law simply shows us how sinful we are."

They have no fear of God and no desire to seek Him.

Without God, mankind is a pretty disgusting mess. This description is of a people who do not have God in their lives and have no desire to know Him—and they have NO excuse for their chosen condition and behavior.

We learned in Chapter two that God created each one of us with an inkling of right and wrong—His moral law. Then He gave His written law to Moses and the Jewish people which is recorded in the Scriptures— leaving no room for doubting that mankind is guilty of sin and in need of a savior.

No matter how hard one may try to follow the law, the "Guilty" verdict will still stand. The law was not meant to rescue the guilty, only to convict. Until the need for rescuing is embraced, the Savior will not be sought.

For those who recognize their guilt and seek God's forgiveness, He promises to reward them. (Hebrews 11:6) "For everyone who asks, receives. Everyone who seeks, finds. And to everyone who knocks, the door will be opened." (Matthew 7:8)

Jesus said, "I am the door. If anyone enters by Me, he will be saved..." (John 10:9 HCSB)

By His grace, God personally offers us the way to have our "Guilty" verdict changed to "Innocent" before Him. We must choose to believe and trust in Jesus Christ as our Savior. He will not only forgive us, He will declare us "Righteous" as He drapes us in His Son's robe of righteousness. (Isaiah 61:10)

28

CHALLENGE: *Doing* good or *being* good may make us *feel* better, but it doesn't make us right with God. Being one with God can only happen by putting our faith in His Son, Jesus.

READ: Ephesians 2:8-9 and Galatians 2:16. What can we tell someone who believes they will go to heaven by following the Ten Commandments?

READ: Acts 13:38-39 – Restate these verses in your own words.

DAY 20

3:21-23 – "But now God has shown us a way to be made right with him without keeping the requirements of the law, as was promised in the writings of Moses and the prophets long ago. We are made right with God by placing our faith in Jesus Christ. And this is true for everyone who believes, no matter who we are. For everyone has sinned; we all fall short of God's glorious standard."

"But now..." The message that followed those two words changed the world for all eternity.

Before... God's righteousness was His and His alone.

Before... Regular blood sacrifices were required to temporarily *cover* the sins of the people.

Before... One must obey God's written Law to be *kept* in right standing with Him.

Before... Only the Jewish people had a special covenant with God.

But now... Because of God's grace, He has chosen to share His righteousness with those who put their faith in His Son.

But now... Our sin has been permanently *removed*—once and for all—through the sacrifice of Jesus on our behalf.

But now... By God's grace and through faith in Jesus, we are *forever* made right with Him.

But now... Both Jews *and* Gentiles are invited into a new covenant with God.

AND GOD DID IT ALL!!!

God created us with a desire for eternal life. (Ecclesiastes 3:11)

God planted in our hearts a conscience that can discern right from wrong. (Romans 2:14-15)

God gave us His written Law and with it came the knowledge that all have sinned and none measures up to His holy standard.

God sent His Son to be the sacrifice for sin—my sin, your sin, yesterday's sin, tomorrow's sin—one perfect, acceptable sacrifice *for all* and *for all time.*

God made it possible for us to share in *His* righteousness. When we accept His free gift of eternal life in Christ Jesus, we are changed from wearing our own unrighteousness to being robed in *His* righteousness. (Isaiah 61:10)

And *God revealed* all this marvelous truth to us *through the prophets and the Scriptures*—holding nothing back. *He wanted* us to know how to be united with Him for all eternity.

Who could reject such love?

CHALLENGE: Since *God has revealed* to us in His Word how to be forever reconciled to Himself—how to live, how to love, how to have joy, peace, contentment, wisdom, understanding, forgiveness, direction, healing, purpose, and HOPE…why would we look or search elsewhere?

READ: John 3:19-21, II Corinthians 4:3-4, and John 12:42-43. Explain why some people reject God and His offer of salvation.

31

DAY 21

3:24-25 - "Yet God, with undeserved kindness, declares that we are righteous. He did this through Christ Jesus when he freed us from the penalty for our sins. For God presented Jesus as the sacrifice for sin. People are made right with God when they believe that Jesus sacrificed his life, shedding his blood. This sacrifice shows that God was being fair when he held back and did not punish those who sinned in times past; for he was looking ahead and including them in what he would do in this present time. God did this to demonstrate his righteousness, for he himself is fair and just, and he declares sinners to be right in his sight when they believe in Jesus."

"Yet God… For God… with God… that God…" These two verses are packed full of truth about the character of God.

We often get so excited about how the message affects us, that we fail to see how much of God's heart is behind it.

We begin here by seeing His grace. We were permanently separated from Him because of our sin. *Yet God*, through Jesus Christ, removed our sin, made us right with Him and took away that separation. Why did He do this? Just because!

Not because we earned it or deserved it. He did it just because He loved us, just because He chose to, just because He is God and therefore, the only One who could. This is *God's Grace*.

Next we see Him "presenting" Jesus—delivering Him up as the sacrifice for our sin. He knew all that would be involved in His Son's horrific death. He also knew that the time would come when He would be forced to turn His back on Jesus and look the other way. But His *holiness* and *justice* required payment for sin so God the Son personally paid the penalty on our behalf—a penalty that cost Him everything. *This is God's Love*.

When we consider all God has done to secure our salvation, and how little effort it takes on our part to receive it, it never seems quite fair. Yet, this is God's plan—the Good News—and as partakers of His grace, we have the opportunity and responsibility of showing the world who God is and what He is like by letting Him be seen in us. The Word says, "We love Him because He first loved us." (I John 4:19) By letting others know of His love for them, they have the opportunity of responding to that Love by putting their faith in Jesus Christ.

CHALLENGE: We can be a good representative of God or a bad one. The better we know Him, the more we love Him. The more we love Him, the more we desire to be like Him. The more like Him, the better representative of Him we become.

READ: Philippines 1:20 – What was Paul's desire concerning his life?

READ: II Corinthians 5:20 – How does this verse define our purpose?

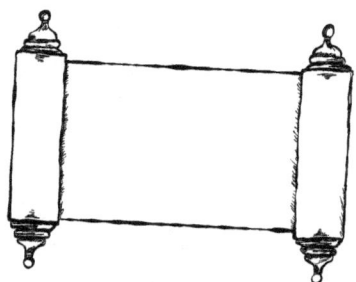

DAY 22

3:25-26 – For God presented Jesus as the sacrifice for sin. People are made right with God when they believe that Jesus sacrificed his life, shedding His blood. This sacrifice shows that God was being fair when He held back and did not punish those who sinned in times past; for He was looking ahead and including them in what He would do in this present time. God did this to demonstrate His righteousness, for He himself is fair and just, and He declares sinners to be right in His sight when they believe in Jesus."

Have you ever wondered what happened to those poor Old Testament people who never had a chance to know and accept Jesus as their savior?

When we say God is fair and righteous we are not simply speaking of Him "being" fair and righteous. We are proclaiming that His character—His very nature—has no ability to be anything other than perfectly fair and perfectly righteous. Therefore, if God extends His grace and mercy to us today, we can be sure He did so in the past as well. If He has made a way for us to be declared righteous, we can be sure He did not exclude those in times past from having the same opportunity.

The scriptures say, "The Father sent the Son to be the Savior of the world." (I John 4:14) His justice and fairness encompasses all mankind; past, present, and future.

In our time, we are made righteous by *having faith* in what God *has done* for us. However, our ancestors were made righteous by *having faith* in what God *promised to do* for them. God demonstrated His fairness and righteousness—and might I add, His mercy—by pardoning Old Testament believers based on the fact that He would *one day* send His Son as the sacrifice for sin—one sacrifice, for all, for all time.

We had no way back to God unless He Himself provided it.

He did so by graciously presenting His own son as the payment for our sin. When we, by faith, accept the free gift of Jesus' sacrifice on our behalf, we gain *His* righteousness—the only way to be made right with God. For Jesus said, "I am the way, the truth, and the life. No one can come to the Father except through me." (John 14:6)

CHALLENGE: If we skip over chapters while reading a book, we will lose out on knowing or understanding the plot and story line. When we study the Scriptures, we must look at the big picture—times past, present, and future—to fully see and understand God's plan for mankind. When we do, hope replaces fear.

READ: Psalm 130:5-8 – Who was David counting on and what had he put his hope in?

READ: I Peter 1:10-12 – Describe what these verses are saying and how they support today's passage.

From these verses how can we know the Old Testament saints were included in God's redemptive plan?

DAY 23

3:27-31 – "Can we boast, then, that we have done anything to be accepted by God? No, because our acquittal is not based on obeying the law. It is based on faith. So we are made right with God through faith and not by obeying the law. After all, is God the God of the Jews only? Isn't He also the God of the Gentiles? Of course He is. There is only one God, and He makes people right with himself only by faith, whether they are Jews or Gentiles. Well then, if we emphasize faith, does this mean that we can forget about the law? Of course not! In fact, only when we have faith do we truly fulfill the law."

If we could be declared righteous by simply following the Ten Commandments, why did Jesus have to die?

Paul reiterates over and over again that we are made right with God through faith in Jesus Christ—not by obeying the law. No matter how sincere and committed we may be in doing what is good and right, it's still trusting in our own effort—focusing on what WE DO. This is *works* and opens us up to pride and self-satisfaction—the trap that stops us from seeking God and His way to forgiveness and eternal life.

The Scriptures say that without the shedding of blood there is no forgiveness of sin.

(Heb. 9:22) In Revelation 1:5 we read, "All glory to Him (Jesus Christ) who loves us and has freed us from our sins by shedding His blood for us." Whether Jew or Gentile, all have the same God and the same way of being made right with Him.

Jesus has done ALL that was required for us to receive forgiveness, redemption, and righteousness. It is *through* Him that we are invited into a personal relationship with God *through faith that comes from HIM!* (I Timothy 1:14)

Through faith in Jesus Christ, God's law of faith has been fulfilled...it is finished.

CHALLENGE: Just *having faith* is not enough. We must have faith **in** Jesus Christ alone to be made right with God.

READ: James 2:19-20 – What do these verses say about just having any kind of faith?

36

READ: Hebrews 11:1 – We cannot confidently hope in something that has no power, ability, or authority to make it happen. Record what this verse tells us about faith and explain how God is needed to give faith the power to act.

DAY 24

4:1-8 – "Abraham was, humanly speaking, the founder of our Jewish nation. What did he discover about being made right with God? If his good deeds had made him acceptable to God, he would have had something to boast about. But that was not God's way. For the Scriptures tell us, 'Abraham believed God, and God counted him as righteous because of his faith.' When people work, their wages are not a gift, but something they have earned. But people are counted as righteous, not because of their work, but because of their faith in God who forgives sinners. David also spoke of this when he described the happiness of those who are declared righteous without working for it; 'Oh, what joy for those whose disobedience is forgiven, whose sins are put out of sight. Yes, what joy for those whose record the Lord has cleared of sin.'"

We don't gain faith through our actions; our actions prove our faith exists.

Let's not be too hard on the Jewish people. For centuries they had done it one way—according to the Law. They basked in the knowledge that God had promised to bless them through their founding father, Abraham. With their eyes on him and the Law they dug in their heels against this new way of finding favor with God through faith.

Paul knew their mindset; he too had been trained in the "good works" kind of righteousness—doing good to *become* righteous instead of doing good *because* you are righteous. He turns their attention to the fact that Abraham believed God *because* he had faith in Him—he trusted Him. In turn, God approved of his faith and declared him to be righteous.

Paul points to another hero of their heritage. King David experienced first-hand the joy of forgiveness because *he believed God*. He trusted God's judgment, His justice, and His grace. He knew he neither earned nor deserved God's favor. (Psalm 32:1-2, Psalm 23) As with each of us, righteousness is the result of God's grace and our faith in Him.

CHALLENGE: Mankind still tries to be acceptable to God apart from having faith in Him. There are those who give large amounts of money to their church, those who pride themselves on their church membership or work hard at community service believing these will win them favor with God. Some believe following the Ten Commandments will get

38

them to heaven. Like Paul and the other Apostles, we must be diligent in sharing the Truth with those who are lost and don't realize it.

READ: Isaiah 64:6 – How does God see righteous acts that are performed apart from His grace and faith in Him?

READ: James 2:18-20 – What do these verses say about works and faith?

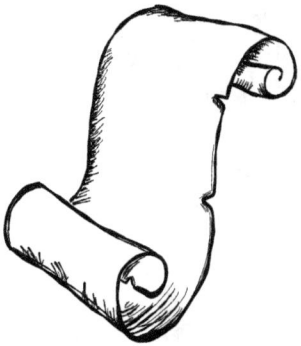

DAY 25

4:9-12 – "Now, is this blessing only for the Jews, or is it also for uncircumcised Gentiles? Well, we have been saying that Abraham was counted as righteous by God because of his faith. But how did this happen? Was he counted as righteous only after he was circumcised, or was it before he was circumcised? Clearly, God accepted Abraham before he was circumcised! Circumcision was a sign that Abraham already had faith and that God had already accepted him and declared him to be righteous—even before he was circumcised. So Abraham is the spiritual father of those who have faith but have not been circumcised. They are counted as righteous because of their faith. And Abraham is also the spiritual father of those who have been circumcised, but only if they have the same kind of faith Abraham had before he was circumcised."

Our driver's license doesn't give us the ability to drive; it's just proof that we can.

Abraham was considered by God to be righteous *before* his circumcision. His obedience in being circumcised was a *sign* of his faith in God.

A good comparison would be baptism. We are not born again *through* baptism—baptism is a *sign* or testimony that we *have been* born again through faith in Jesus Christ.

Abraham's faith in God is legendary. His stories have been read and repeated for generations. He obediently packed up his family and left when God had not even told him where he was going. He obediently built an altar with every intention of sacrificing his son Isaac, only to have the knife's fatal plunge halted by God Himself, in proof of Abraham's faith and obedience.

None of this earned him his righteous standing with God—it was the *evidence of his faith in Him*. Abraham was an example to the world that being made right with God is dependent on having faith in Him—a vital truth in a world where faith is so misplaced and trust fails to be trustworthy.

"Abraham believed God and it was credited to him as righteousness." (Hebrews 9:22)

40

CHALLENGE: Faith must have an anchor—it must be rooted in a source that is infallible, omniscient, and sovereign or it will fail. God is the only anchor that merits our faith.

READ: Hebrews 11:3 – What biblical truths does faith help us understand?

READ: Hebrews 12:2 – Where does our faith come from?

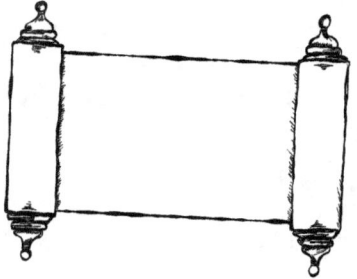

DAY 26

4:13-15 – "Clearly, God's promise to give the whole earth to Abraham and his descendants was based not on his obedience to God's law, but on a right relationship with God that comes by faith. If God's promise is only for those who obey the law, then faith is not necessary and the promise is pointless. For the law always brings punishment on those who try to obey it. (The only way to avoid breaking the law is to have no law to break!)"

Abraham accepted and received God's promise because he believed God would be true to His word.

These verses sum up what Paul had formerly taught: righteousness is a gift based on faith, not on obedience to the Law. We see this in the life of Abraham. He received God's promise because of his faith, not because he followed the Law. If following the Law *could* make one righteous or guarantee God's promise there would be no need for faith…or God's grace.

On the other hand, if we *had to* live our life totally free of sin to be declared righteous, there would be no need for the promise of eternal life because there would be NO recipients. We've already learned in Romans 3:10 that, "No one is righteous—not even one."

God's perfect plan for redeeming mankind is spelled out clearly in Paul's letter to the Ephesians. "For you are saved by grace through faith, and this is not from yourselves; it is God's gift—not from works, so that no one can boast." (Ephesians 2:8-9 HCSB)

We can ONLY receive God's righteousness and His promise of eternal life through faith—by believing He can and will do what He says. He graciously offers us the opportunity of having a relationship with Him through His Son Jesus Christ—a relationship that offers love, forgiveness, peace, joy, power, companionship, wisdom, and eternal life.

When we come to realize that there is one way to be saved—through faith in Jesus Christ—there is no place we would rather be than at His feet.

CHALLENGE: Salvation is a free gift. God paid the price for it and freely gives it to us when we have faith in Jesus Christ. Earning salvation is an impossible task.

READ: I Peter 1:3-5 – What is the basis for our hope? (vs 3) What do we have awaiting us and how certain and secure is it?

4:16-18 – "So the promise is received by faith. It is given as a free gift. And we are all certain to receive it, whether or not we live according to the law of Moses, if we have faith like Abraham's. For Abraham is the father of all who believe. That is what the Scriptures mean when God told him, 'I have made you the father of many nations.' This happened because Abraham believed in the God who brings the dead back to life and who creates new things out of nothing. Even when there was no reason for hope, Abraham kept hoping—believing that he would become the father of many nations. For God had said to him, 'That's how many descendants you will have!'"

We can believe everything God says. Everything!!

God made a promise to Abraham that he would be the father of many nations—that he would have many descendants. *Abraham believed God!* He knew in his heart that he could count on God to make it happen. He received the promise because he had faith in the One who gave it.

We must not miss the importance of this truth. Abraham *knew* it would happen. He wasn't told how or when, but he *knew without a doubt* that it would happen exactly as God said because *he believed whatever God told him.*

God knew Abraham's heart just like He knows ours. The faith that motivated Abraham's belief pleased God. As a result, God declared him to be a righteous man. Not only did He make him the father of the Jewish nation, He made him the father of *all* who have faith in God—namely, us!

It was not and is not the law that makes us one with God's heart and with each other. We are drawn into an eternal relationship with God by possessing faith in Him—the One who created us, redeemed us, and intimately knows the heart of each one of us.

The same believing faith that Abraham had in God is what He desires from us as well. Because God is faithful, like Abraham, we can faithfully believe *everything* He says.

CHALLENGE: Choosing to BELIEVE God goes much deeper than simply believing in God.

READ: John 6:66-69 – What wise conclusion did Peter come to and can you identify with him?

READ: Psalm 119:42,43,89,160 – What do these verses tell us about God's words to us?

DAY 28

4:19-22 – "And Abraham's faith did not weaken, even though, at about 100 years of age, he figured his body was as good as dead—and so was Sarah's womb. Abraham never wavered in believing God's promise. In fact, his faith grew stronger, and in this he brought glory to God. He was fully convinced that God is able to do whatever He promises. And because of Abraham's faith, God counted him as righteous."

Abraham's faith never weakened!

Abraham was 100 years old when Isaac, the promised son of God's covenant, was born. He was seventy-five when God promised to make him a great nation with many descendants. For nearly twenty-five years he waited to see God's promise fulfilled—or at least set in motion. With each passing year he and Sarah grew older and the reality of them having a baby at such advanced ages must have seemed more and more impossible. Yet instead of giving in to doubts or giving up on the promise all together, we're told his faith grew stronger through his test of waiting.

Let's not miss what his steadfast faith ultimately accomplished. It brought glory to God—he actually gave God glory while he waited.

When we believe God, we exhibit faith in His truth, power, faithfulness, and *ability to do what He has promised.* Through our faith and praise, attention is drawn to the glorious character of the Lord. The better we know God, the more our faith grows. The more our faith grows, the more opportunities we have to reflect His glory.

In this "want it right now" world, when we find ourselves in our test of waiting, let's use the time profitably by demonstrating steadfast faith and recognizing the majesty of God.

CHALLENGE: In the process of waiting we must faithfully keep moving toward and with God. Treading water never gets us where we need to be.

READ: Galatians 6:9 – What promise do we find in this verse for our faithfulness while waiting?

READ: Ecclesiastes 3:11 – Explain how this verse can give up hope for the future and patience in our times of waiting.

44

4:23-25 – "And when God counted him as righteous, it wasn't just for Abraham's benefit. It was recorded for our benefit, too, assuring us that God will also count us as righteous if we believe in him, the one who raised Jesus our Lord from the dead. He was handed over to die because of our sins, and he was raised to life to make us right with God."

Our faith has sight behind it.

Abraham was made right with God because he believed Him. This fact was put to pen as an example to us. We, too, can be confident that by having faith in God, we ARE changed from being unrighteous to being righteous. However, we have a precious benefit that Abraham didn't have—we can personally know the Messiah that he was only told of.

It is possible for us to actually see the place where the Son of God died for our sins. We have the privilege of knowing "It is finished!" instead of having to *look forward* to the time when it can be said, "When He sees all that is accomplished by His anguish, He *will* be satisfied. And because of His experience, my righteous servant *will* make it possible for many to be counted righteous, for He *will* bear all their sins." (Isaiah 53:11) (Italics mine)

Abraham had been given this wonderful promise and he believed that God was able to make it happen. We have all the facts and evidence that God DID make it happen; so our faith has much to be rooted in.

We know God spoke directly to Abraham and He speaks to us as well. The Scriptures are His voice—His message to us. His Holy Spirit living within us activates the Scriptures, giving them power to teach us, correct us, equip us, convict us, and ultimately, to grow our faith in Him as we spend time in communion together.

Abraham lived day by day believing God's promise. As believers, we live day by day experiencing His promise.

CHALLENGE: When Jesus said, "It is finished!" He became the door between righteousness and unrighteousness. It is only through faith in Him that we can experience the promise of eternal life.

READ: John 10:9, John 14:6 and Revelation 3:20 – Jesus is speaking in each of these verses. What point is He making in each one and what does it mean to you?

READ: Romans 10:17 – Explain how our faith grows.

DAY 30

5:1-2 – "Therefore, since we have been made right in God's sight by faith, we have peace with God because of what Jesus Christ our Lord has done for us. Because of our faith, Christ has brought us into this place of undeserved privilege where we now stand, and we confidently and joyfully look forward to sharing God's glory."

Our faith unleashes God's grace and glory.

Being right with God is like having a peace treaty with Him. All things between you and God have been reconciled and there is now peace. Creator and creation are one and there is reason to rejoice, for "There is no condemnation for those who belong to Christ Jesus" (Rom. 8:1). This is only made possible because of God's grace.

None of us deserves such kindness—we haven't the ability to earn His forgiveness in order to be right with Him. God offers us forgiveness and eternal life because He chooses to. This is an act of His grace.

When we, by faith, accept His Son as our Savior, He accepts us into His family and we have the joy of sharing His glory. We have the privilege and responsibility of showing the world how glorious God truly is by allowing His character and identity to be seen in and through us. Psalm 19:1 says the "heavens declare the glory of God" and we stand in awe at its splendor. But the children of God are to be His splendor as well, for God says, "Bring all who claim me as their God, for I have made them for my glory." "I will display my holiness through those who come near me. I will display my glory before all the people." (Is. 43:7, Lev. 10:3)

We are holy vessels that contain a great treasure—with confidence and joy, and with the power of the Holy Spirit, let's share this treasure with others.

CHALLENGE: We bear the name of Jesus Christ. Let's be good representatives of Him and for Him.

READ: II Corinthians 5:20-21- Define "Ambassador". What is the message we are to share with the world?

READ: Acts 4:13 – What do we learn about Peter and John in this verse? The last sentence speaks volumes. Explain why.

46

5:3-5 – "We can rejoice, too, when we run into problems and trials, for we know that they help us develop endurance. And endurance develops strength of character, and character strengthens our confident hope of salvation. And this hope will not lead to disappointment. For we know how dearly God loves us, because He has given us the Holy Spirit to fill our hearts with His love."

It's easier to endure difficulty when we know there is benefit in it.

When a woman is in labor and the pain gets unbearable she is often reminded to focus on the grand finale—her little baby. The value in the process of pain can be seen and appreciated, not only for the moment while she holds her baby, but this experience will help her be better equipped for the next painful experience life brings.

In this passage God assures us through the Apostle Paul that our trials are meant to benefit us. However, this can only happen if we allow God to be our deliverer. Jesus said, "My grace is all you need. My power works best in weakness." Paul responded to this truth by saying, "I take pleasure in my weaknesses…when I am weak, then I am strong." (II Cor. 12:8-10)

God never expects us to trust in our own resources. By having HIS life within us, we have HIS power, HIS strength, HIS wisdom, HIS discernment, HIS peace, HIS rest, and HIS hope—absolutely everything we need to endure the trial and be victorious. With each victory, our Beloved Father God becomes more real and more personal to us. His love for us becomes a tangible truth that strengthens our hope of eternal life and all the promises it holds—causing the things of earth to grow "strangely dim".

With Paul, we can have joy in our trials and take pleasure in our weaknesses for the benefits far outweigh the sufferings.

CHALLENGES: Going through trials *without God's help* can bring bitterness or pride—depending on the outcome. Going through them *with* God brings humility, growth in our faith, and glory to God.

READ: II Corinthians 12:7-10 – Why does Paul say he was given the thorn in his flesh?

Was he delivered from this thorn/trial?

Describe Paul's heart and attitude as a result of this trial.

47

DAY 32

5:6-9 – "When we were utterly helpless, Christ came at just the right time and died for us sinners. Now, most people would not be willing to die for an upright person, though someone might perhaps be willing to die for a person who is especially good. But God showed His great love for us by sending Christ to die for us while we were still sinners. And since we have been made right in God's sight by the blood of Christ, He will certainly save us from God's condemnation."

If "hero" is defined as one who is willing to risk or even lose his life to save another, then Jesus Christ is the greatest hero in the history of mankind.

When we were completely cut off from God because of sin...when we were facing eternity in hell with NO hope...when we were utterly helpless to do anything to undo, change, or save ourselves from the situation we were in... *Jesus Christ came to save us!*

He didn't wait for us to clean up our act or do something that would make us worthy of help. In love He just came. *He* reached out to *us*. He told us through His prophets and through His Word that because of our sin, we had a horrible fate awaiting us. Then, *He came.* He gave us hope by taking *upon Himself* our punishment for that sin, by paying the cost that *HIS own righteousness* required—by offering forgiveness and freedom to all who would trust in Him. Motivated by love, He did it all so we didn't have to remain cut off from Him. He didn't want anyone to be destroyed because of their sin. (II Peter 3:9)

Do you believe this? Have you accepted God's offer of forgiveness and salvation from the penalty of sin? Are you allowing Him to be the loving Lord over your life...your future...your eternity?

I mean this in the most respectful and honorable way. Jesus Christ is the greatest hero of all time. He has saved more people from a dreadful fate than anyone in human history. He saved me and is my Hero. He wants to be yours as well. Have you said yes to His offer?

"I pray that God, the source of hope, will fill you completely with joy and peace because you trust in Him. Then you will overflow with confident hope through the power of the Holy Spirit." (Romans 15:13)

CHALLENGE: If you knew where a door of escape was in a burning building, you would certainly tell others the way out. We must look at Jesus Christ and His Good News in this light.

READ: Luke 4:42-43 – Why does Jesus say He preaches the Good News?

READ: Exodus 9:16 – Explain how this verse can motivate us to share the Gospel.

DAY 33

5:10-11 – "For since our friendship with God was restored by the death of His Son while we were still His enemies, we will certainly be saved through the life of His Son. So now we can rejoice in our wonderful new relationship with God because our Lord Jesus Christ has made us friends of God."

Sometimes we need to go back to the beginning to be able to appreciate fully the here and now.

God said, "Let us make human beings in our image, to be like us." So He created mankind in His own image. He looked at what He had made and saw that it was "very good". He placed man in the Garden of Eden to tend and watch over it. Both man and his wife were naked, but *they felt no shame.*

The Lord God warned them, "You may freely eat the fruit of every tree in the garden—except the tree of the knowledge of good and evil. If you eat its fruit, you are sure to die."

Now, the serpent was the shrewdest of all the animals God had made, and one day he told the woman, "You won't die? God knows that your eyes will be opened and you will be like God, knowing both good and evil." Desiring it, the woman was convinced so she took some of the fruit and ate it. Then she gave some to her husband, who was with her and he ate it. Suddenly, their eyes were opened and *they hid* themselves from God. For the first time, *they felt shame*—innocence was lost! Mankind was now at odds with its Creator. (Genesis 1-3)

Disobedience and sin had fractured the relationship between God and mankind—making them enemies. But God, full of love and by His grace, made a way for us to be reconciled to Him. Through the death of His Son, our relationship with God is restored. We no longer have to hide from God but can "rejoice in our wonderful new relationship with Him." Because of Jesus Christ, we are no longer enemies, but "friends of God."

Our fractured relationship with God has been healed by the blood of Jesus Christ!

This is Good News...is it not?

CHALLENGE: Being a friend of God means having a deep desire for Him and for spending time with Him.

READ: Psalm 62:5-6, 63:1-5 – What do these verses tell us about David and how can they be an example to us?

READ: James 2:23 – Who was a friend of God and why?

DAY 34

5:12-15 – "When Adam sinned, sin entered the world. Adam's sin brought death, so death spread to everyone, for everyone sinned. Yes, people sinned even before the law was given. But it was not counted as sin because there was not yet any law to break. Still, everyone died—from the time of Adam to the time of Moses—even those who did not disobey an explicit commandment of God, as Adam did. Now Adam is a symbol, a representation of Christ, who was yet to come. But there is a great difference between Adam's sin and God's gracious gift. For the sin of this one man, Adam, brought death to many. But even greater is God's wonderful grace and His gift of forgiveness to many through this other man, Jesus Christ."

All humanity bears the mark of its first representative—all possess Adam's "sin DNA" and deserve to die.

Adam, the progenitor of the human race, sinned, and death became the universal consequence. Once man's eyes were opened to the knowledge of evil, there was no going back. Innocence was lost, and to this day the seed or nature of sin is being passed on in the heart of all mankind generation after generation. Therefore, all are guilty before God because of this inherited sin nature and all carry the death penalty. Just as the entire football team gets penalized when one player crosses the skirmish line before the ball is hiked, all mankind suffers the penalty for one man's sin.

This seems like extreme injustice, and it would be if it ended here. But God is *just* and as the *Creator of justice*, He took it upon Himself to *justify* the situation. He sent His one and only Son to pay the penalty for ALL—ALL who accept His offer of *justification* through faith are declared innocent and receive a righteous standing before God. We learned this in Romans 3:24, "Yet God, with undeserved kindness, declares that we are righteous. He did this through Christ Jesus when he freed us from the penalty for our sins."

By the act of one man, Adam, all were made unrighteousness...but by the act of one man, Jesus Christ, all can be made righteous. This time we have a choice!

Many years ago, by faith I chose to believe God—I accepted His offer of forgiveness through His Son Jesus Christ—I gave Him my heart, my life, and my eternity. He gave me the forgiveness He had promised and added His righteousness, hope, and eternal life. He became my Savior, my Lord—my constant companion. By His grace He is my purpose for living.

CHALLENGE: The choice is ours. What decision have you made concerning the Lord Jesus Christ?

READ: Acts 4:12, John 3:36 – Explain how these verses declare there is only one way to be made right with God and for receiving the gift of eternal life.

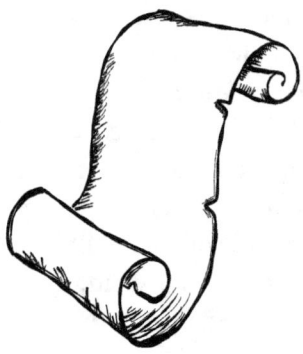

DAY 35

5:16-19 – "And the result of God's gracious gift is very different from the result of that one man's sin. For Adam's sin led to condemnation, but God's free gift leads to our being made right with God, even though we are guilty of many sins. For the sin of this one man, Adam, caused death to rule over many. But even greater is God's wonderful grace and His gift of righteousness, for all who receive it will live in triumph over sin and death through this one man, Jesus Christ. Yes, Adam's one sin brings condemnation for everyone, but Christ's one act of righteousness brings a right relationship with God and new life for everyone. Because one person disobeyed God, many became sinners. But because one other person obeyed God, many will be made righteous."

This time we do have a choice—we can receive by faith or reject the results of Jesus' act of redemption.

These verses invite us to explore the differences between the act of the first man, Adam, and the act of the man, Jesus Christ. Both acts affected the entire human race—one negatively and one positively. Both deliberately chose their act in full knowledge of the result. When we look at how each act affected our relationship with God, we see a vast difference.

Looking first at the result of Adam's disobedience to God's command not to eat of the tree of the knowledge of good and evil, we see it allowed man to know and understand evil for the first time. Innocence was lost and the heart of man was stained with sin, making him unrighteous and causing a separation between him and his righteous Creator. True to God's word, death became the enemy of mankind and sin became his master. In himself, man had no power to stand against it or change his unrighteous condition—He was without hope.

Now, looking at Jesus' act of obedience to His Father's plan for the forgiveness and redemption of mankind, we see it freed man from the power of sin and removed its stain from his heart. By His grace, God declared man innocent and gave him—as a special gift—His Son's righteousness. Through Jesus' act the required death penalty was paid in full and man received the promise of eternal life. To guarantee His promise and to supply the power needed to resist sin, God chose to "move in" to man's heart to personally and permanently dwell with him through His Spirit. Man now has hope!

Going from being guilty to innocent…unrighteous to righteous…from being separated from God, to being made right with Him…from being powerless, to having power…from being hopeless, to having hope…from death, to life everlasting *for "all who receive it"*. The sacrificial act of Jesus was God's grace in action—providing the way to bring us back to Him.

However, there is another "act" required…this time it's ours to choose. We must believe and receive the invitation for redemption offered by God through His Son Jesus Christ.

CHALLENGE: A gift must be received and accepted before it becomes ours.

READ: John 1:12 – How do we become children of God?

READ: John 5:24 – When do we receive eternal life?

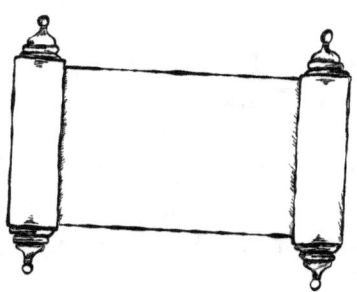

DAY 36

5:20-21 – God's law was given so that all people could see how sinful they were. But as people sinned more and more, God's wonderful grace became more abundant. So just as sin ruled over all people and brought them to death, now God's wonderful grace rules instead, giving us right standing with God and resulting in eternal life through Jesus Christ our Lord."

We cannot fully embrace the Good News until we are convinced and shaken by the bad news.

God has never tried to keep the sinfulness of man's heart a secret. He told us in Romans 3:23 that everyone is a sinner and in Romans 3:10 that there is no one who is righteous…not even one. Jeremiah 17:9 says, "The human heart is the most deceitful of all things, and desperately wicked." It is in direct contrast with God's heart and that is the *bad news*.

When we come to understand and accept the bad news, God's grace goes into action. He lovingly begins to draw us to Himself by revealing to us His wonderful *Good News*. "Christ died for our sins, just as the Scriptures said. He was buried, and He was raised from the dead on the third day, just as the Scriptures said." (I Cor. 15:3-4) "For God loved the world so much that He gave His one and only Son, so that everyone who believes in Him will not perish but have eternal life." (John 3:16) "So now there is no condemnation for those who belong to Christ Jesus. And because you belong to Him, the power of the life giving Spirit has freed you from the power of sin that leads to death." (Rom. 8:1)

Now that is Good News!! And there is more…. The Bible is full of good news. It tells us all about our great God and our Savior, Jesus Christ. It explains God's plan for mankind, and through it the Holy Spirit reveals God's individual plans for you and me. The Scriptures are the source of knowing God and understanding the hope we have in Jesus Christ.

CHALLENGE: Our newspapers are full of bad news—why not spend time in God's Word and read some Good News.

Contrasting the good news with the bad news:
I Peter 2:9 - Going from darkness to _____.
Colossians 2:13 – You were _____. God made you
_____.

56

Luke 19:10 – Christ seeks and saves those who are _____.

Romans 15:4 – The Scriptures give us _____ and _____.

Matthew 11:28 – All who are _____ He will give you _____.

DAY 37

6:1-4 – "Well then, should we keep on sinning so that God can show us more and more of His wonderful grace? Of course not! Since we have died to sin, how can we continue to live in it? Or have you forgotten that when we were joined with Christ Jesus in baptism we joined Him in His death? For we died and were buried with Christ by baptism. And just as Christ was raised from the dead by the glorious power of the Father, now we also may live new lives."

The more we sin the more grace is required on God's part. However.....

Like a naughty child who requires more attention and patience from the parents, more grace and cleansing blood is required for the child of God who continually sins. So the thinking *might be*, "Let's sin a lot so we can experience an abundance of God's grace."

I've often wondered if someone actually suggested this to Paul or if he was merely exercising the "nipping it in the bud" idiom. Whatever the case, he strongly rejects the very idea of such an atrocity against the Lord. How ludicrous to test the grace of God and dishonor the blood of Jesus in such a way.

As followers of Jesus we are joined together with Him and separated from sin and its power over us. Through baptism we identify ourselves with His death and resurrection—dying to sin and living a new and victorious life. This is how the power of His blood is proven and the grace of God is magnified—not to mention the gift of joy that is given to those who obey God.

"Joyful are those who obey His laws and search for Him with all their hearts." (Psalm 119:3)

CHALLENGE: Looking at sin lightly *devalues* the sacrificial blood of Jesus and the grace of God.

READ: I Samuel 15:22 – What does this verse say concerning obedience?

READ: I Peter 1:14-15 - How are we supposed to live?

READ: Hebrews 10:29 – How do you think we can trample on Jesus Christ and His blood?

58

6:5-8 – "Since we have been united with Him in His death, we will also be raised to life as He was. We know that our old sinful selves were crucified with Christ so that sin might lose its power in our lives. We are no longer slaves to sin. For when we died with Christ we were set free from the power of sin. And since we died with Christ, we know we will also live with Him."

We are no longer powerless against sin and its pull on us.

When Christ died, He broke the power of sin—it has no power to control or condemn us. We are no longer slaves to "self-rule" and sinful desires. We don't *have to* sin!

I John 3:9 says, "Those who have been born into God's family do not make a practice of sinning because God's life is in them." Having God's life within us gives us the privilege and authority to draw on His power in times of temptation. Again, we don't *have* to sin—it's our *choice* and responsibility to draw close to God in times of temptation to gain victory over sin's pull. By choosing to do so, our heart remains soft and open to His voice and our close relationship with Him is maintained. We can enjoy His presence moment by moment.

Our *new life* with Him needs to be nurtured. Being alive with Christ is a *position* that will never change. However, keeping our new life in good *condition* before God is our responsibility. We must be sensitive to the Holy Spirit's warnings and quickly go to Him for protection and power when facing any sinful temptation.

We are no longer bound to the power of sin and its consequences. We have the ability to live abundantly as we take refuge in Jesus Christ.

CHALLENGE: Our temptation to sin will come when we least expect it and in our weakest areas. We must be alert, prepared, and in full armor—God will do the rest. (Ephesians 6:10-17)

READ: I Peter 5:8, James 4:7 – These verses speak of our enemy—the devil, Satan. What instructions do they give concerning him?

READ: I John 4:4, 5:4, I Corinthians 10:13, and Proverbs 21:31. What do these verses tell us about temptation and having victory over it?

DAY 39

6:9-11 – "We are sure of this, (that we will live with Christ-see verse 8), because Christ was raised from the dead, and He will never die again. Death no longer has any power over Him. When He died, He died once to break the power of sin. But now that He lives, He lives for the glory of God. So you also should consider yourselves to be dead to the power of sin and alive to God through Christ Jesus."

Sin no longer has the power to condemn us if Jesus Christ is living within us.

Unlike the Old Testament sacrifices that needed to be performed over and over again to cover the people's sin, Jesus Christ died **once**. He was the perfect sacrifice that paid the penalty for **all** sin. Sin no longer has the power to condemn those who are in Christ Jesus. God says it like this. "For sin is the sting that results in death, and the law gives sin its power. But thank God! He gives us victory over sin and death *through our Lord Jesus Christ.*" (I Cor. 15:57) Because of Christ, we are spiritually alive and sin can no longer bring spiritual death to us. We are eternally forgiven! That my friend is eternal security!

The blood of Jesus Christ was so perfect and powerful that it paid the price for *every* sin that *every* person commits—past, present, and future. However, we must *individually* believe in Jesus Christ and accept His gracious offer of forgiveness. By doing so, we die to the power of sin and Jesus Christ enters our heart and life to dwell with us eternally. Because of this new fellowship, we will never again be separated from Him because of sin.

Again, God says it like this. "So now there is no condemnation for those who belong to Christ Jesus." (Rom. 8:1) Eternally alive in Him!! Aren't you glad you are His and He is yours?

CHALLENGE: Sin has no power to condemn us—only cripple us.

READ: Psalm 32:3, 66:18, Isaiah 59:2 – What do these verses say about unconfessed sin?

READ: I John 2:1, I John 1:9, and Psalm 32:1 – What results from confessing our sin?

60

6:12-14 – "Do not let sin control the way you live; do not give in to sinful desires. Do not let any part of your body become an instrument of evil to serve sin. Instead, give yourselves completely to God, for you were dead, but now you have new life. So use your whole body as an instrument to do what is right for the glory of God. Sin is no longer your master, for you no longer live under the requirements of the law. Instead, you live under the freedom of God's grace."

When we are devoted to Jesus Christ He instills Godly desires into our heart and then gives us the power and free will to live them out.

Psalm 37:4 says, "Take delight in the Lord, and *He will give* you your heart's desires." In Galatians 5:17 we're told that *the Spirit gives* us desires that are the opposite of what the sinful nature desires. When we allow sin to control us, *our desires come from sin* and are contrary to God—and because we cannot serve two masters, we become slaves of sin rather than slaves of Jesus Christ.

It takes a conscious decision to forsake sin and surrender to God's authority. Once this is done, we can live free in His grace.

I once heard a story about a puppy that lived in a fenced in yard. He had everything he needed for living a happy, carefree life. Inside his fence he was fed, loved, protected, and free to do and be whatever his little heart desired. But outside his fence lurked dangers that could cause him great harm. He could get lost or stolen. He could get hit by a car or poisoned—he could starve. For this puppy, freedom meant remaining inside his fence.

This is a good picture of life for the obedient child of God. Living *within His righteous standards* gives us freedom to do and be whatever we desire— because it is God planting the desires within us and His grace fencing us in. There is no better place to be!

CHALLENGE: We must exercise our freedom in Christ in ways that honor Him and demonstrate to those around us the joy and fulfillment found in living in obedience to Him.

READ: Psalm 40:8 – David found joy in obedience to God. What prompted his obedience?

READ: I John 2:6 – How does John say we should live our lives?

READ: Colossians 3:17 – What truth does Paul use in this verse to challenge us to live in obedience to God?

6:15-18 – "Well then, since God's grace has set us free from the law, does that mean we can go on sinning? Of course not! Don't you realize that you become the slave of whatever you choose to obey? You can be a slave to sin, which leads to death, or you can choose to obey God, which leads to righteous living. Thank God! Once you were slaves of sin, but now you wholeheartedly obey this teaching we have given you. Now you are free from your slavery to sin, and you have become slaves to righteous living."

We may not be "slaves" *to* sin but we can still be "enslaved" *by* sin.

Sin has no authority to control us unless we submit to it. As we have already learned, we don't have to sin. Having God's life within us has given us victory over the power and condemnation of sin. However, if we *choose* to play with sin, we will not be protected from its consequences.

God's grace and our new life in Him is eternal—we cannot be stolen away from God by sin or the evil one. But we can create an unhappy household in our heart and life if we choose to invite sin in for a visit. The Holy Spirit within will not be a welcoming host—*there will be consequences.*

The conviction we begin to experience at this time is the Spirit's way of turning our focus and heart back to our Heavenly Father, where forgiveness and righteousness reign. Choosing righteousness over sin will prove to be a valuable decision when we realize the rewards that come with it. Forgiveness and unity with God, freedom from a guilty conscience, peace of mind, confidence in our walk and talk—the *unleashing of God's power*—are just a few of the blessings that come with obedience.

There are some who reject being under the control of someone else… let's not be one of them. Especially when the ONE in control is the One who created us…the One who died for us…the One who lives for us and is preparing a place for us. He IS wisdom, He IS love… Why would we want our life controlled by anything or anyone other than the ONE who owns the universe—the King of all Kings—the Lord of all Lords!

CHALLENGE: Giving control of our life to God frees us from having to deal with the consequences that come from allowing "self" to have control.

READ: John 15:4 – How successful can we be in our spiritual life without God's control?

READ: Jeremiah 10:23 – Jeremiah makes two profound statements here. What are they?

DAY 42

7:1-4 – "Now, dear brothers and sisters—you who are familiar with the law—don't you know that the law applies only while a person is living? For example, when a woman marries, the law binds her to her husband as long as he is alive. But if he dies, the laws of marriage no longer apply to her. So while her husband is alive, she would be committing adultery if she married another man. But if her husband dies, she is free from that law and does not commit adultery when she remarries. So, my dear brothers and sisters, this is the point: You died to the power of the law when you died with Christ. And now you are united with the one who was raised from the dead. As a result, we can produce a harvest of good deeds for God."

"Until death do us part."

Paul is using an example here that the people knew and understood to help them see they were no longer bound to the law. When they "died with Christ", their covenant with God through the law was broken; just as a marriage covenant is broken when one partner dies. Now they were bound to—united with—Christ Jesus in a new covenant. It was no longer a covenant written in stone, it was one written on their heart through the indwelling life of Christ.

For all those who put their faith in Jesus, His death was credited to them *through* their faith and *by* God's grace—in the same way Christ's righteousness is credited to us. They died to the old covenant—their old life—and have a new covenant—a new life in Christ.

This new covenant began after Christ's resurrection and ascension, on the day of Pentecost, when the Spirit of God came to dwell with and in God's people. It's by the Holy Spirit's power and presence that the world can see godly fruit in the life of a believer. Our desire is to do good deeds that help further the gospel and the building of His kingdom.

We may not be bound to the law, but Jesus said He didn't come to do away with the law but to fulfill it. (Matt.5:17-18) It's moral and ethical teaching will be valuable and make its mark as long as there is a heaven and earth.

CHALLENGE: The Law *told* us how one should live—Jesus came and lived out the Law; *showing* us how one should live.

READ: Hebrews 7: 23-24 and 9:15 – Why is the new covenant—forgiveness through the blood of Jesus—better than the old covenant—the Law?

In the Sermon on the Mount (Matt. 5) Jesus quotes the Law several times and then adds, "But I say.....". (See 5:21-22, 5:27-28, 5:31-32, 5:38-39) Explain how Jesus' words "fulfill" the Law.

65

DAY 43

7:5-6 – "When we were controlled by our old nature, sinful desires were at work within us, and the law aroused these evil desires that produced a harvest of sinful deeds, resulting in death. But now we have been released from the law, for we died to it and are no longer captive to its power. Now we can serve God, not in the old way of obeying the letter of the law, but in the new way of living in the Spirit."

Being told "Don't" tends to make people want to "Do".

When the old nature is in control, sinful desires run amuck and the ability to resist them is nearly non-existent—leaving a trail of sin and spiritual death.

The law was meant to reveal sin—to raise red flags in the heart of man in an attempt to persuade him to do good and not evil. However, the flesh—being rebellious by nature—sees the law as a taunting challenge to *do* what it says *not to*. Around it goes. The law says, "NO"...the flesh says, "YES". But the law, the standard for righteousness brings guilt upon the offender who is in captivity to the old nature.

It appears to be a hopeless situation!

"But now..." Hope comes with these two words from verse six that announce the release from the law and introduce the "new way of living in the Spirit".

Having the Spirit of God living in us not only gives us power to resist sin and its pull on us, but the law—being the very character of God—is in us. When surrendered to God, *His life* and character will be exhibited as His Spirit interacts with ours and the character of the law is lived out in *our life*.

The law, for the Believer, is not a chain around the neck, but is a gathering of principles that kept the Old Testament brethren current with God and can be a map for living a life pleasing to Him as we allow His Spirit to exercise control over us.

We obey God—not the law. We are saved through faith—not the law. But the law will always be a valuable blueprint for living a righteous life.

CHALLENGE: Do we live in obedience to God because we love him, or do we live in obedience because it's the way we've been taught to live? A heart full of love for God will respond to His heart and will. Learned

66

behavior may cause one to *do* right but doesn't necessarily mean the heart is right with God.

READ: Matthew 23:27-28 – What was missing in the heart of the Pharisees in this passage?

READ: Luke 6:45, Proverbs 4:23, and Proverbs 21:2 – Explain why the heart condition is so important in our Christian walk with Christ.

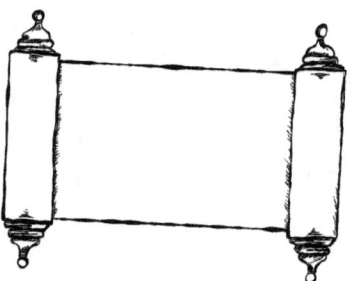

DAY 44

7:7-9 – "Well then, am I suggesting that the law of God is sinful? Of course not! In fact, it was the law that showed me my sin. I would never have known that coveting is wrong if the law had not said, "You must not covet." But sin used this command to arouse all kinds of covetous desires within me! If there were no law, sin would not have that power. At one time I lived without understanding the law. But when I learned the command not to covet, for instance, the power of sin came to life, and I died."

How would we know we're speeding if there were no speed limit signs?

Paul claims he would not have known he was sinning if the law had not told him what sin was. Even then, sin—almost with a mind of its own—working together with his flesh, brought about temptations that would never have come to light if they had not been motivated by the law.

Back to our speed limit signs…if we didn't know the speed limit was fifty-five, we wouldn't be *tempted to break the law* by setting our cruise control on sixty—hoping the officers of the law would forgive us for only being five over. Here is the formula: **Sin** uses the *law* (speed limit 55) to **tempt and motivate the flesh**'s "need for speed", **to sin** by breaking the law when setting the cruise on sixty.

Does this make the law wrong? Of course not!! However, it can stir us up to react either right or wrong. We can resist the temptation, or we can give in to it. Paul looks at "giving in" as death, with sin being the victor. We know that Paul holds nothing back and has declared himself the chief of sinners. (I Tim. 1:15) He understands that the old nature leans toward sin. But we are not left powerless!! We have the life of Christ living in us and His power at our fingertips.

Being released from the law does not mean we no longer have a need for it. It simply means it has no power to condemn us. The law represents the will and character of God, so it is important to Him. Jesus came to fulfill the law—to live it out before the world—and He did it *perfectly*. As we desire to grow and become more like Him, we, too, can be representatives of our God. With His life within us, we have the power and ability to be victorious over the world. Remember, He has already won the battle.

CHALLENGE: The law was needed to stir and convict the conscience of sin and wrong. Now we have the Spirit of God living within us to remind us of His righteousness and our responsibility to be like Him.

READ: John 16:5-8 – These verses explain the working of the Holy Spirit. How did the law do this before the Spirit's coming?

GALATIANS 5:16-18 – Describe the battle going on in these verses and how we can have victory through the battle.

DAY 45

7:10-14 –"So I discovered that the law's commands, which were supposed to bring life, brought spiritual death instead. Sin took advantage of those commands and deceived me; it used the commands to kill me. But still, the law itself is holy, and its commands are holy and right and good. But how can that be? Did the law, which is good, cause my death? Of course not! Sin used what was good to bring about my condemnation to death. So we can see how terrible sin really is. It uses God's good commands for its own evil purposes. So the trouble is not with the law, for it is spiritual and good. The trouble is with me, for I am all too human, a slave to sin."

We must see the need for change and desire that change before it will happen.

Man is born facing spiritual death because he is born with a sinful nature. The law exposes or brings to light the sin that exists in mankind, thereby bringing guilt and death to all offenders. Paul says he was one of these victims. The law told him what was right and good—how to live righteously—but it also showed him he was not able to follow or obey it perfectly because he was a sinner. Therefore, he was guilty before God and spiritually dead.

The very thing that was meant to set him on the right path to God revealed he was on the path to destruction.

Paul saw himself correctly. Like all possessors of the human nature, his natural instincts leaned toward sin. The law, with its commands on how to be righteous, simply showed him how unrighteous he was. Did this mean the law was a bad thing? Absolutely not! If not for the law, he would not have seen his sin and his need for a savior.

Like Paul, we must first see our sin and the need to be forgiven and freed from the penalty of it. Only then will we see our need for a Savior—Jesus Christ.

His death on our behalf is the only payment acceptable for our forgiveness because *only a perfectly righteous sacrifice could bring righteousness.*

God had to pay the penalty Himself!!

God set the standard according to His own character.

We broke the standard—Sin leading to death.

Jesus paid the price for our sin and guilt—His death on the cross.

70

Have you accepted His offer of forgiveness and *life*? For "the free gift of God is eternal life through Christ Jesus our Lord." (Rom.6:23b)

CHALLENGE: Our perception of God must be balanced. We must recognize His righteousness and justice as well as His love and forgiveness.

READ: Psalm 119:137-138 and 145:17 – What do these verses tell us about God and His law?

READ: Psalm 9:7-8 and Proverbs 29:26 – What do these verses tell us about justice?

71

DAY 46

7:15-20 – "I don't really understand myself, for I want to do what is right, but I don't do it. Instead, I do what I hate. But if I know that what I am doing is wrong, this shows that I agree that the law is good. So I am not the one doing wrong; it is sin living in me that does it. And I know that nothing good lives in me, that is, in my sinful nature. I want to do what is right, but I can't. I want to do what is good, but I don't. I don't want to do what is wrong, but I do it anyway. But if I do what I don't want to do, I am not really the one doing wrong; it is sin living in me that does it."

They call it "good intentions"…

Paul is sharing with us a personal struggle that we can all identify with—wanting to do good but not doing it, and not wanting to do bad, but doing it anyway. He does not say he has conquered his battle—quite the contrary. Several times he says, "I can't", and "I don't", in reference to doing what is right; which is what he desires to do but keeps failing.

He makes an important point in verse sixteen when he says he *knows* what he's doing is wrong. The law is serving its purpose by revealing to Paul his sin and wrong doing. This proves the law is a good thing. However, he had to *know* the law before it could do its work in his heart.

This is also true for us in regards to the Scriptures. We must *know* God's Word before its transforming power can be unleashed in our heart and life to bring about conviction, repentance, and spiritual maturity. The Spirit cannot remind us of certain Scriptures *when we need them* if we never knew them in the first place. We must know God's Word before we can obey it, grow from it, find encouragement and joy in it, and practice the instructions and standards it contains.

Paul's problem was not that he didn't know right from wrong, for he knew the law inside and out. It was the spiritual war raging *inside him*—God's holy nature battling with Paul's sinful nature for dominance over his heart that caused him such frustration. This is the very same war we fight.

Good and evil have always been at odds. Sin and righteousness are old enemies and the battle between the two will continue to plague the life of believers until we are safely with the Lord. Until then, sin will do all it can to hinder us, cause us to fall, discourage us, weaken us, bring about doubt and fear, and the most damaging of all, cause us to give up. Left to ourselves, we don't have a chance. However, God has provided the power to fight and win each battle if we will only surrender them to Him. He has told us in I John 4:4, "…the Holy Spirit who lives in you is greater than the spirit who lives in the world." Victory will be ours when we allow the Spirit of the Lord Jesus Christ, living within us, to fight the battles on our behalf. We just have to ask Him….then trust Him.

CHALLENGE: We may feel like we never get it right—but remember, we're not alone in the battle.

READ: Acts 13:22 – How is David described here?

READ: Psalms 51:1-3 – Describe David's plea in these verses.

READ: I Samuel 16:7 – What comfort can be found in this verse?

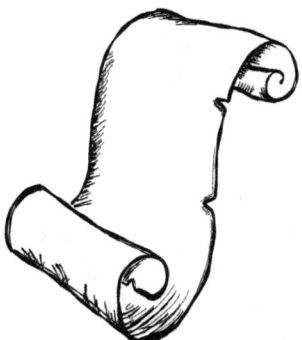

73

DAY 47

7:21-25 – "I have discovered this principle of life—that when I want to do what is right, I inevitably do what is wrong. I love God's law with all my heart. But there is another power within me that is at war with my mind. This power makes me a slave to the sin that is still within me. Oh, what a miserable person I am! Who will free me from this life that is dominated by sin and death? Thank God! The answer is in Jesus Christ our Lord. So you see how it is: In my mind I really want to obey God's law, but because of my sinful nature I am a slave to sin."

"God's law is written in their hearts." (Romans 2:15)

We learned in the second chapter of Romans that God created each of us with an instinctive moral law—the sense to know right from wrong. However, without the Holy Spirit within us, it's difficult to go against our natural desires to do what is right or not do what is wrong. We are often tempted to give in to it.

Paul found that once the Holy Spirit came into his life, war broke out between his own sinful spirit and the perfect, sinless Spirit of Jesus Christ. His mind said, "Do this…", but his sinful nature said, "Don't do this…". Sound familiar? He was disgusted by this war raging within him. But as the light of Truth turned on in his heart, he saw his hope—he saw the answer. It is "in Jesus Christ our Lord."

No matter how fierce the battle and how weak our resolve, the constant presence of our Savior Lord is our hope and answer. Calling on Him unleashes *His* defense and *His* strength to turn the battle in our favor *for His glory*. No conflict is too vicious, no temptation so strong, that the power of God cannot and will not handle it *on our behalf*. Our job is to *let Him!*

Jesus said, "My power works best in weakness." to which Paul replied, "That's why I take pleasure in my weakness… For when I am weak, then I am strong." (II Cor. 12:9-10)

It's human nature to try to handle our own conflicts—there's a sense of pride if we can successfully come out on top. But oh, what we miss when we choose to bypass God. We miss the opportunity to experience His faith-building divine power; a treasure we may find useful in the next go around. Most of all, we miss the opportunity to reflect His glory.

"He does this to make the riches of His glory shine even brighter on those to whom He shows mercy, who are prepared in advance for glory."

"Then all of you can join together with one voice, giving praise and glory to God, the Father of our Lord Jesus Christ." (Rom. 9:23, 15:6)

This is why we are here!!!

CHALLENGE: A battle fought and won through the power and presence of God *brings Him glory*. When we strive to do it alone, *pride* can be a dangerous enemy.

READ: I Chronicles 21:1-3, 21:7-8 – Why do you think David took the census and why was God displeased with it? What can we learn from David's sin?

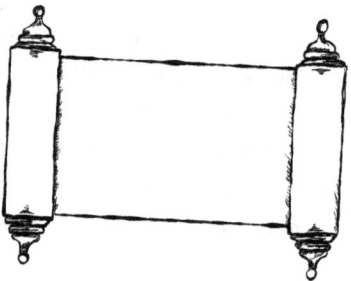

75

DAY 48

8:1-3 – "So now there is no condemnation for those who belong to Christ Jesus. And because you belong to Him, the power of the life-giving Spirit has freed you from the power of sin that leads to death. The law of Moses was unable to save us because of the weakness of our sinful nature. So God did what the law could not do. He sent His own Son in a body like the bodies we sinners have. And in that body God declared an end to sin's control over us by giving His Son as a sacrifice for our sins."

We are no longer "guilty" before God—our Judge. We have been acquitted! How did this happen?

Jesus claimed our sin as His own and then willingly gave up His life in payment for our crimes—freeing us from *all* guilt, past, present, and future.

God knew this was something the law could not do, so He sent His Son, Jesus, into our world to represent mankind. To do so, He had to *be* mankind—so He came to us in human flesh. He lived among us, growing "in wisdom and in stature and in favor with God and all the people." (Luke 2:52) He revealed His deity through the miracles He performed and the amazing words He spoke. He did this so we would believe in Him—learn to trust Him—put our faith in Him—and receive Him as our own beloved Savior and King. This was the only way that sin, with its over-powering pull on us, could be crushed and broken and we could receive forgiveness.

With the Spirit of Jesus living within us, we have help saying "no" to sin and wrong and "yes" to those things that please Him and benefit us and others. I have found that each time I call on Him for help, He faithfully gives it. It causes my love *for* Him and my faith *in* Him to grow.

Jesus paid the cost for our acquittal. When He said, "It is finished," while hanging on the cross, the Judge's gavel came down, declaring that there is no longer any condemnation for those who are in Christ Jesus—the verdict is now "not guilty". However, it did not end there. He didn't save us and leave us to stand alone. The Scriptures tell us that *now* He faithfully holds our right hand and will never leave us. He is constantly present with us. (Psalm.73:23, Isaiah 41:13)

Only the God of the universe could, by His righteousness, declare His creation guilty of sin and deserving of death, and then—by His grace and love—send a Kinsman Redeemer to free all who believe in Him of their

76

guilt and eternal punishment. AND THEN, choose to live in and with them, providing them with His strength, His wisdom, and His companionship each and every moment for the rest of their natural life—meanwhile, preparing a special place in Heaven for each of His children. WHO DOES THAT??? Only our God, the King of Kings and Lord of Lords, *our* Lion of Judah, *our* Ancient of Days, the Darling of Heaven, our Saving Friend, King Jesus.

CHALLENGE: When God says there is no judgment for believers, He means it. It is finished!! Jesus took care of it and we must not let the enemy tell us anything different.

READ: John 3:18 and Isaiah 43:25 – Explain how eternal life began the moment we accepted Christ as our Savior.

77

DAY 49

8:3b-8 – God declared an end to sin's control over us by giving His Son as a sacrifice for our sins. He did this so that the just requirement of the law would be fully satisfied for us, who no longer follow our sinful nature but instead follow the Spirit. Those who are dominated by the sinful nature think about sinful things, but those who are controlled by the Holy Spirit think about things that please the Spirit. So letting your sinful nature control your mind leads to death. But letting the Spirit control your mind leads to life and peace. For the sinful nature is always hostile to God. It never did obey God's laws, and it never will. That's why those who are still under the control of their sinful nature can never please God."

We each have a decision to make!

Like the Apostle Paul, we struggle with the battle of wills. Our old nature desires to have control over our heart. But the Holy Spirit's presence and voice is a strong reminder to be obedient to the will of God and submit to His control. For if we allow our old nature to have control, our thinking, ultimately our behavior will be "hostile" to God.

Paul gave this message to the church at Galatia: "So I say, let the Holy Spirit guide your lives. Then you won't be doing what your sinful nature craves." He goes on to say that when we allow the Holy Spirit to have control, HE will give us "desires that are the opposite of what the sinful nature desires." (Gal. 5:16-17) King David said these similar words: "Take delight in the Lord and He will give you your heart's desires." (Ps. 37:4)

We like to think this means if we delight in the Lord, the Corvette we've always wanted is going to miraculously appear in our driveway. But what God is actually saying is that if our heart finds its delight in the Lord Jesus Christ, He will instill within us the desires *He wants there*—desires that are in unity with His.

Being one with God will lessen the battles with our old nature and multiply our victories over it. However, as long as we are in these bodies, the enemy will be pounding on our heart's door trying to get control. This is where our responsibility of decision making comes into play. Are we going to hand over the controls to the Lord or to the enemy?

When my daughter was about four years old I was trying to teach her this spiritual truth—complex even for adults. When I caught her disobeying a long-standing rule, her explanation was, "God's Spirit told me not to do it, but my spirit wanted to do it. Today, I listened to my spirit." I'm sure we can all identify with this dilemma. But the more control we give to the Holy Spirit, the more victories He will win on our behalf.

CHALLENGE: Never give up! *Choosing* to obey God's Spirit automatically puts our spirit and will in submission to Him.

READ: John 3:30-31 – What are these verses saying to you?

DAY 50

8:9-11 – "But you are not controlled by the sinful nature. You are controlled by the Spirit if you have the Spirit of God living in you. (And remember that those who do not have the Spirit of Christ living in them do not belong to Him at all.) And Christ lives within you, so even though your body will die because of sin, the Spirit gives you life because you have been made right with God. The Spirit of God, who raised Jesus from the dead, lives in you. And just as God raised Christ Jesus from the dead, He will give life to your mortal bodies by this same Spirit living within you."

It's all about life and living.

There are some things that God chooses to keep us in the dark about; such as His second coming. In these cases, we just have to trust Him and believe in His sovereign wisdom and will. But there are other things that He urgently wants us to know and understand. We find them repeated often in the Scriptures. One of these vital truths concerns the resurrection of the dead.

The Scriptures tell us Jesus would be raised from the dead. (Mark 8:31, Luke 24:46) David said God would not allow His "holy One to rot in the grave." (Ps. 16:10) Job said he knew his Redeemer lived and he would see Him with his own eyes. (Job 19:25-27) Jesus Himself told His disciples that "The Son of Man *will be* betrayed to the leading priests and the teachers of religious law. They *will* sentence Him to die. Then they *will* hand Him over to the Romans to be mocked, flogged with a whip, and crucified. But on the third day He *will be* raised from the dead." (Matt. 20:18-19)

Paul records the fulfillment of Christ's words in I Corinthians 15:3-4. "I passed on to you what was most important and what had also been passed on to me. Christ died for our sins, just as the Scriptures said. He *was* buried, and He *was* raised from the dead on the third day, just as the Scriptures said." Paul goes on to say, "We know that God, who raised the Lord Jesus, *will also raise us* with Jesus and present us to Himself together with you." (II Corinthians 4:14)

This speaks of *our* resurrection from the dead. Jesus said, 'I am the resurrection and the life. The one who believes in Me, even if he dies, will live. Everyone who lives and believes in Me will *never die—ever*." (John 11:25-26) (all emphasis mine)

In today's passage we see it was the Spirit of God who raised Jesus from the dead—the same Spirit who now lives in us. He is our *guarantee* of being resurrected from the dead *to continue on* in heaven with Jesus Christ our Savior; for our eternal life began the moment we received Him into our heart and life.   This truth is a huge boulder in the spiritual foundation for hope.

CHALLENGE: Consider…Death is not the end of *life* for the believer—nor is it the beginning.

READ: John 3:36 and John 5:24 – Both of these verses mention *eternal life*. Is it something we WILL possess or something we DO possess?

READ: I John 1:1-2, and I John 2:24-25 – How is our eternal life connected to our relationship with Jesus Christ?

81

DAY 51

8:11b-14 – "…He will give life to your mortal bodies by this same Spirit living within you. Therefore, dear brothers and sisters, you have no obligation to do what your sinful nature urges you to do. For if you live by its dictates, you will die. But if through the power of the Spirit you put to death the deeds of your sinful nature, you will live. For all who are led by the Spirit of God are children of God."

Freedom is having no walls between you and God.

When sinful thoughts or attitudes rise up and attempt to stir us to sinful behavior or activities, we are under no obligation to listen and obey. We owe no allegiance to our sinful nature. For if we continually cave in or cater to the demands and wooing of our "self"—ignoring the tugs of the Holy Spirit—we slowly kill our sensitivity to the voice of God and can become hard-hearted. (Hebrews 4:7, James 1:15, I Thess. 5:19)

Brick by brick we build a wall between God's Holy Spirit and our heart that can and will eventually shut out the Spirit's voice and influence over us. Once again, we become a slave to the sinful desires from which the Spirit of God came to free us. Our hearts and minds become easy targets for the enemy's deception, temptation, and twisting of truth.

But we belong to God!! Jesus Christ has won the victory on our behalf.

Through repentance and obedience to God's will we can once again experience the "still small voice" of our beloved Savior—gaining freedom from the pulling chains and desires of our sinful nature. The wall will come down and the Spirit of God can once again steer our heart away from sinfulness and toward righteousness.

Belonging to God gives us the freedom to say "no" to our own desires and "yes" to the voice and leading of His Spirit.

CHALLENGE: The choice to listen and obey is ours to make. God will never force Himself on us.

READ: Luke 11:28 and James 1:25 – What is promised to us if we obey God and His word?

READ: Isaiah 1:19 and Deuteronomy 11:22-23 – What blessings were promised to Israel if they would obey God?

8:15-17 – "So you have not received a spirit that makes you fearful slaves. Instead, you received God's Spirit when He adopted you as His own children. Now we call Him, "Abba, Father." For his Spirit joins with our spirit to affirm that we are God's children. And since we are His children, we are His heirs. In fact, together with Christ we are heirs of God's glory. But if we are to share His glory, we must also share His suffering."

The Holy Spirit is God's down payment on the glory He wants to share with us.

Having God's Spirit living within us is not meant to cause us fear. His role is not one of a heavy-handed task master forcing us to behave against our will.

God chooses to live with us so He can encourage and comfort or instruct and admonish when needed—to give us peace in times of trouble and remind us of what He has taught us. He guides us with His wisdom and discernment and gives us warning and strength so we can have victory over temptations. He is our faithful companion who desires the very best for us, as a father does for his child.

God's Spirit is the living proof that we have been adopted by God and are now His child—making us joint-heirs with Jesus and giving us the right and privilege to call Him "Father".

Having the Spirit of God guarantees our eternal inheritance. He IS our resident hope of receiving all that God has promised. The Scriptures tell us: "I am going to prepare a place for you… When everything is ready, I will come and get you, so that you will always be with me where I am." (Eph. 1:14, John 14:1-4) Be assured, Jesus means what He says.

Our Father has not left us to fend for ourselves. "By His divine power, God has given us everything we need for living a godly life." (II Peter 1:3) God did this by sending His Spirit to live in the heart of all those who belong to Him.

This does not mean all will be peaches and cream for us. We are reminded in our passage for today that even though we can expect to share in God's glory, we must also realize that suffering is and will be a part of life. Jesus experienced it and so will we. However, like Jesus, we don't have to go it alone. The Holy Spirit has all the power to get us through. We just have to ask Him, trust Him, and then allow Him to do His work in and through us.

CHALLENGE: The indwelling of the Holy Spirit is a precious gift that we must NEVER take for granted or over look.

READ: Ephesians 1:13 and John 14:26 – The Spirit is at work in us. What does He do as our resident power and Advocate?

READ: John 14:15-17 – Who gives us the Holy Spirit? Is this a permanent relationship? What does Jesus mean when He says, "He lives with you now and later will be in you."?

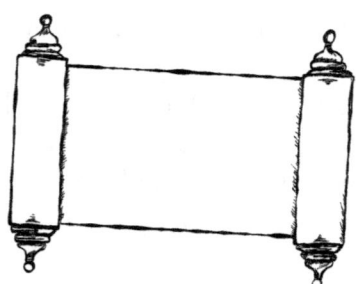

DAY 53

8:18-23 – "Yet what we suffer now is nothing compared to the glory he will reveal to us later. For all creation is waiting eagerly for that future day when God will reveal who His children really are. Against its will, all creation was subjected to God's curse. But with eager hope, the creation looks forward to the day when it will join God's children in glorious freedom from death and decay. For we know that all creation has been groaning as in the pains of childbirth right up to the present time. And we believers also groan, even though we have the Holy Spirit within us as a foretaste of future glory, for we long for our bodies to be released from sin and suffering. We, too, wait with eager hope for the day when God will give us our full rights as His adopted children, including the new bodies He has promised us."

Our troubles don't disappear when we become a child of God.

As joint heirs with Jesus we have a share in His glorious inheritance; but we also have a share in his suffering—and suffering has many faces.

Believers in regions that outlaw Christianity may have to endure imprisonment or the loss of their life or the life of a loved one. Others may suffer physically with vicious diseases or debilitating handicaps. Some may have to watch with hands tied while sin wreaks havoc or destroys the life of a beloved family member or friend. No one is exempt from trouble and suffering because no one is exempt from the consequences of living in a fallen world.

The earth itself pays the penalty of man's sin. Death and decay, earthquakes and hurricanes, tornadoes and volcanoes were not realized in Eden. They are evidence of a world tainted by sin—a world that eagerly waits to be restored to its first created beauty and harmony.

But still, Paul says all this suffering will seem like nothing compared to the awesome, glorious inheritance that awaits us.

Every trophy that sits on a shelf or rests in a place of honor represents a challenge that has been overcome. Eternal life is the prize for which we fight for and endure.

In new bodies we will enjoy the treasures of heaven with its streets of gold, gates of pearl, foundation of gems, and crystal clear river flowing through an orchard of life giving fruit trees. But best of all, the throne of God will reside in the center and Jesus Christ, the risen sacrificial Lamb will meet with us face to face—the One who made all this possible. (Rev. 21)

Paul said, "I press on to reach the end of the race and receive the heavenly prize for which God, through Christ Jesus, is calling us." (Phil. 3:14)

CHALLENGE: Our temporary sufferings and troubles will fade in the light of the glory that God will surround us with one day.

READ: Mark 8:31, Luke 24:26, 46 – Jesus knew He would endure sufferings. Who spoke of it earlier?

READ: II Corinthians 1:5, I Peter 5:10, and Hebrews 11:26 – There are rewards in enduring sufferings. We don't endure them alone. What can we look forward to from suffering?

8:24-25 – "We were given this hope when we were saved. (If we already have something, we don't need to hope for it. But if we look forward to something we don't yet have, we must wait patiently and confidently.)

We don't have to wait not knowing…

The moment we were saved God's Spirit moved in and took up residency in our heart—putting God's personal seal on us. (Eph. 1:13) His life in us is our *hope*—our guarantee of having eternal life. Therefore, we *know* what awaits us.

We *know* what our new home will be like and look like. (Rev.21:10-27) We *know* Jesus Christ and many other friends and family members will be there. (Acts 1:9-11) We *know* it all began the moment we received the Spirit of God into our heart and life. (Galatians 4:6)

Until this future inheritance is *fully* realized, we wait and do the work we were called to do. (Eph. 2:10) We look forward to experiencing the rest of our story—knowing God will faithfully keep His promises. (Hebrews 10:23)

In the meantime, we have a job to do. We live, serve, experience, and journey on as representatives of Jesus Christ—confidently *knowing* where the journey will ultimately lead us: into the presence of our Savior and Lord *forever!*

Our eternal inheritance is a sure thing. *Hope* is a gift God has given to help us through the struggles and hard times of waiting. We know our Redeemer lives and is preparing a place for us where we can forever enjoy the blessings that come from being His. (John 14:1-4)

CHALLENGE: Live your life with eternity as your focus—basking in the Light of Heaven.

READ: I John 5:13, John 5:24 and John 11:25-26 – These verses tell us we can know we HAVE eternal life. How does this knowledge affect our daily life?

READ: Ephesians 2:18-20 and Philippians 3:20 – What do these verses tell us and how can they affect our daily life?

DAY 55

8:26-27 – "The Holy Spirit helps us in our weakness. For example, we don't know what God wants us to pray for. But the Holy Spirit prays for us with groanings that cannot be expressed in words. And the father who knows all hearts knows what the Spirit is saying, for the Spirit pleads for us believers in harmony with God's own will."

We are not alone in our prayers!

These verses continue on with the subject of groaning. We groan, waiting for the end of our battle with unrighteousness and the fulfillment of our promised, glorious inheritance. The earth groans in its fallen, chaotic state; desiring the perfect beauty of its original masterpiece. And in these verses God shares a great mystery with us concerning the groanings of His Holy Spirit on our behalf.

As human beings we are weak. We can't see the same way God sees. We have no way of knowing all He knows. We can't foresee the extent or purpose of every issue that confronts us. So when we come to our Father in prayer, we come with limited sight—talking to Him about what we *do know*. However, the Holy Spirit, who knows our heart and understands our weakness also knows and understands the heart and will of God. He sees past the surface of our prayer and goes to the very core of the issue where it relates to God's ultimate will. On our behalf, He labors over our hearts desires with words that only the Father understands; reconciling those desires with God's own will. He goes far beyond what we ask or think.

In Christ Jesus we have a great High Priest and advocate who knows our weaknesses and pleads our case before the Father. (Heb. 4:15, I John 2:1) We also have living in us the Holy Spirit, who shares our deepest heart desires with the One who loves us most. Why then would we ever hesitate when it comes to praying? Why would we ever doubt its effectiveness?

God said, "The earnest prayer of a righteous person has great power and produces wonderful results." (James 5:16)

"So take courage! For I believe God. It will be just as He said." (Acts 27:25)

CHALLENGE: When we underestimate the power of prayer we underestimate the power and participation of the Holy Spirit.

READ: John 14:13-14 and Exodus 3:13-14 – We are to pray in Jesus' name. Jesus is God. God told Moses His name was "I AM WHO I AM". In other words, His name WAS who He WAS. We must know Him—His character, His heart, His will. Only then are we fully able to pray in His name—identifying with His character, in sync with His heart, and aligned with His will. The Holy Spirit takes it from there.

89

DAY 56

8:28-30 – "And we know that God causes everything to work together for the good of those who love God and are called according to His purpose for them. For God knew His people in advance, and He chose them to become like His Son, so that His Son would be the firstborn among many brothers and sisters. And having chosen them, he called them to come to Him. And having called them, He gave them right standing with himself. And having given them right standing, He gave them His glory."

When watching a parade we only see what's before us at any particular moment.

God has a master plan for mankind that encompasses thousands of years. It weaves its way through generation after generation and His purposes even now are being orchestrated in your life and mine. Nothing has ever happened that God did not have former knowledge of or a hand in, and nothing that He has planned for tomorrow can be changed, halted, or bypassed. (Job 42:2, Isaiah 14:27)

The good news is that every bit of our life for Christ is for our ultimate good, and when it's all played out, the evidence of God's love, grace, wisdom, righteousness, and justice will be clearly seen.

In the meantime, as we struggle to see the good in some things and the reasons for others, we live by faith—believing and trusting in the One who created all things and whose character and ways are always good and kind. King David said, "The Lord is righteous in *everything* He does; He is *filled* with kindness." (Psalm 145:17 emphasis added)

God is not forced to *work around* the sin, disappointments, and horrors that come from living in a fallen world. He chooses to *work with* them to grow us, mold us, test us, nurture us, strengthen us, and ultimately teach us that "Without Him we can do nothing." (John 15:5)

When we get to this point of discovery, true wisdom—God's wisdom—settles us. We see the need to fully surrender to Him and trust His omniscience, sovereignty, and love.

This is the example Jesus set for us while He walked *in our shoes* and died *on our soil.*

90

CHALLENGE: God's goal and desire for His people is to become more and more like His Son. Surrendering to His wise authority is the beginning.

READ: I Corinthians 13:12 – How can this verse help us surrender to God and His plan?

READ: Isaiah 41:4 and 46:9-10 – How can these verses give us hope and reassurance?

READ: John 5:30 and John 14:31 – Explain how Jesus' words can be an example to us today.

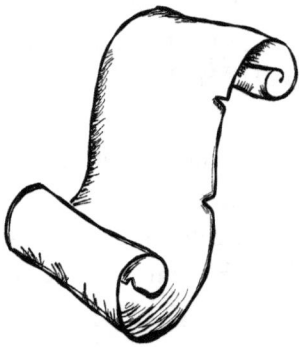

DAY 57

8:31-34 – "What shall we say about such wonderful things as these? If God is for us, who can ever be against us? Since He did not spare even His own Son but gave Him up for us all, won't He also give us everything else? Who dares accuse us whom God has chosen for his own? No one—for God Himself has given us right standing with Himself. Who then will condemn us? No one—for Christ Jesus died for us and was raised to life for us, and He is sitting in the place of honor at God's right hand, pleading for us."

"If God is for us, who can ever be against us?" Who indeed??

These verses imply that there are those who will oppose us, accuse us, and try to bring condemnation on us. God assures us, however, that **their efforts will fail** because Jesus is the One who has already won the war. We have an arsenal of power and promises, for the Scriptures tell us:

- *God* has chosen us to be His very own – Titus 2:14, "He gave His life to free us from every kind of sin, to cleanse us, and *to make us His very own people*, totally committed to doing good deeds." I Peter 2:9, "…you are a chosen people. You are royal priests, a holy nation, *God's very own possession.*"

- *God* has put His seal/mark on us – Ephesians 1:14. "The Spirit is God's guarantee that He will give us the inheritance He promised and that He has purchased us to be His own people." II Corinthians 1:22. "He has identified us as His own by placing the Holy Spirit in our hearts as the first installment that guarantees everything He has promised us."

- *God* purchased us with the blood of His Son Jesus – I Peter 1:18-19. "For you know that God paid a ransom to save you from the empty life you inherited from your ancestors. And the ransom He paid was not mere gold or silver. It was the precious blood of Christ, the sinless, spotless Lamb of God."

- *God* gives us the strength we need to fight the battles – Psalm 46:1. "God is our refuge and strength, always ready to help in times of trouble." Isaiah 12:2 – "See, God has come to save me. I will trust in Him and not be afraid. The LORD God is my strength and my

92

song; He has given me victory." Philippians 4:13. "For I can do everything through Christ, who gives me strength."

- *God* goes before us and behind us – Psalm 139:5, "You go before me and follow me. You place your hand of blessing on my head." Deut. 31:8. "Do not be afraid or discouraged, for the LORD will personally go ahead of you. He will be with you; He will neither fail you nor abandon you."

CHALLENGE: We must stop living like victims of the enemy. God has won the war and He is our power and Protector.

READ: II Peter 1:3-4 and answer the following questions.

What does God's divine power enable us to do?
How did we receive this power?
What can this power help us do?

READ: II Timothy 3:16-17 – What role does Scripture play in our arsenal of power and promises?

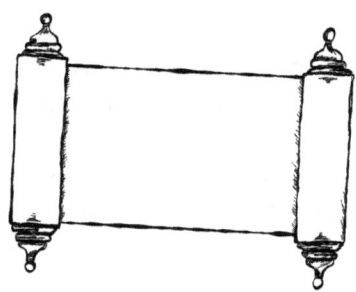

93

DAY 58

8:35-37 – "Can anything ever separate us from Christ's love? Does it mean He no longer loves us if we have trouble or calamity, or are persecuted, or hungry, or destitute, or in danger, or threatened with death? (As the Scriptures say, "For your sake we are killed every day; we are being slaughtered like sheep.") No, despite all these things, overwhelming victory is ours through Christ, who loved us."

"Comfort and prosperity have never enriched the world as much as adversity has." (Billy Graham)

When trouble, trials, and hard times plague us, it's easy—almost natural—to believe God has abandoned us. Our head may say, "He will never leave us or forsake us", but the feelings of abandonment want to take over.

The Apostle Paul told Timothy that everyone who wants to live a godly life in Christ Jesus will suffer persecution. He then challenged him to remain faithful to the things he had been taught because he knew they were true. (II Tim. 3:12-14) Paul's counsel can inspire us in the same way it did Timothy. In hard times we must hold on to what we know is true based on God's Word.

We know God loves us and is faithful. (Lam. 3:22-23) We know He will give us wisdom when we ask for it, strength to do all things, and that He is the source of ALL hope, joy and peace. (Jms 1:5, Phil. 4:13, Rom. 15:13) We know we can take refuge in Him and have overwhelming victory through Him *because He has overcome the world.* (Ps. 46:1, John 16:33)

Our trials will be used by God to get us to where we need to be. They will drive us to Him and cause us to examine our heart—often leading to repentance or the need to let go, rest in Him, and let Him do His work. Our brother Joseph clung to this truth when—in reference to what his brothers had done to him—he said to them, "You intended to harm me, but God intended it all for good." (Gen. 50:20)

God is too wise to make mistakes and loves us too much to be unkind. We can fully, faithfully trust Him!

CHALLENGE: When we begin to feel defeated, beat down, alone and unloved, we must make the same claim Paul did. NO!!! Overwhelming victory is mine *through Jesus Christ*!!

READ: Psalm 119:71 and record a benefit that can come from our suffering.

READ: I Peter 1:6-7 – What will be proven through your trials and what will be the results?

How can this truth be of encouragement to you?

DAY 59

8:38-39 – "And I am convinced that nothing can ever separate us from God's love. Neither death nor life, neither angels nor demons, neither our fears for today nor our worries about tomorrow—not even the powers of hell can separate us from God's love. No power in the sky above or in the earth below—indeed, nothing in all creation will ever be able to separate us from the love of God that is revealed in Christ Jesus our Lord."

Absolutely nothing can separate us from God's love for us.

Based on his personal experience Paul clung to this truth with such conviction that nothing could sway him to believe otherwise. In the wake of his persecution of Christ's followers he was unconditionally loved and forgiven by Jesus Christ Himself. He learned that there is nothing so final, fierce, or powerful that God's love will not hold fast in the face of it.

If more proof is needed, we only need to consider the horrible death and victorious resurrection of Jesus.

God's plan for redeeming us from sin's curse was set in motion the day His Son took His first breath as a human baby in that stable in Bethlehem. Driven by His love for us, the Father orchestrated the life and ultimate sacrificial death of His beloved Son on our behalf. It is through HIS death and resurrection three days later that we can obtain forgiveness from our sin and gain the hope of eternal life WITH HIM.

God's great love for us is spelled out in the words of John 3:16. "For God loved the world so much that He gave His one and only Son, so that everyone who believes in Him will not perish but have eternal life."

I'm sorry that Jesus had to die for me—but I'm so grateful that He loved me enough to say, "My Father! If it is possible, let this cup of suffering be taken away from me. Yet I want your will to be done, not mine."

It was ALL done because of God's unconditional, inseparable love for you and me!

CHALLENGE: God's love for us can be measured by the death and life of His Son.

READ: Jeremiah 31:35-37 – What do these verses tell us about God's devotion to His people?

READ: Ephesians 2:4-7 – What proof of God's love for us do we see in these verses?

9:1-3 – "With Christ as my witness, I speak with utter truthfulness. My conscience and the Holy Spirit confirm it. My heart is filled with bitter sorrow and unending grief for my people, my Jewish brothers and sisters. I would be willing to be forever cursed—cut off from Christ!—if that would save them."

"…if that would save them." But Paul knows there's absolutely no hope in that ever happening.

Paul's heart was heavy over the unbelief of his fellow Jews. God's Spirit within him lamented in harmony with Paul's at their rejection of Jesus. Paul believed Jesus was the Messiah and accepted His teachings as truth. He believed that being made right with God could only be achieved by God's grace and through faith in His Son Jesus Christ. He had become one of Jesus' most passionate followers.

It broke his heart that his people could not/would not accept the good news of this new covenant with God but chose to hold on to the old one represented by the law. He knew that following the law could not save them and was willing to do whatever it took to win his people—even if it meant *changing places with them.*

This is a very noble and convicting example for us to identify with. Does our passion for lost souls drive us to such heights? Paul loved his people and longed for their acceptance of Jesus as their Messiah Savior. Still today the nation of Israel as a whole has not embraced the truth- that the son of Joseph the carpenter was and is the Son of God—their Messiah.

Paul was sent by God to preach the Good News to the Gentiles; however, he did not lose his desire to see salvation come to his fellow Jews. (Eph. 3:1-2) He hoped they would witness the Gentile's acceptance of God's gift of grace and become jealous of the relationship they found with God through the Lord Jesus Christ. (Rom. 11:13-14) Paul never gave up on his Jewish people—his heart stretched big enough to include the Gentiles.

CHALLENGE: We must never stop trying. We must never give up on those around us who are lost. We have the answers that can give them the hope for which they are desperately searching.

READ: Isaiah 49:6 – How could this verse have encouraged Paul?

READ: Ephesians 3:8 – How did Paul see his assignment of preaching to the Gentiles?

READ: Galatians 2:9 – Who partnered with Paul in ministering to the Gentiles and who focused their ministry on reaching the Jewish people?

CONSIDER: Was God pouring out His mercy on Paul by sending him to the Gentiles, knowing that he would experience rejection by his own people? Do you think that Paul found any comfort in knowing that Jesus Himself, along with His message had also been rejected by the Jews?

9:4-5 – "They are the people of Israel, chosen to be God's adopted children. God revealed His glory to them. He made covenants with them and gave them His law. He gave them the privilege of worshiping Him and receiving His wonderful promises. Abraham, Isaac, and Jacob are their ancestors, and Christ Himself was an Israelite as far as His human nature is concerned. And He is God, the One who rules over everything and is worthy of eternal praise! Amen."

The Jewish people and their country have held the world's eye for centuries—not often to their benefit.

The people of Israel were God's select group of people—not because they earned it or deserved it. Their position was their privilege only by the sovereign grace and will of God. He made it possible for them to know Him. He allowed them to experience His power, protection, direction, love, and forgiveness. He made promises to them that He faithfully fulfilled from generation to generation. His desire was for them to love Him and worship Him only. Did this happen? Off and on—more off than on. Yet still, He loved them and was faithful to them.

It was through these people that God would bring salvation to the world. His only begotten Son was born human with Jewish flesh and blood. He would be the Lion of Judah, the King of Kings and Lord of Lords. He would personally spread the news of His coming kingdom—proving His identity claims with miraculous deeds and works of healing; both physical and spiritual. Ultimately, it would be to these people that He would surrender Himself. He would go "as a sheep to the slaughter" to be beaten, abused, and crucified at their bidding.

These are the people of the Apostle Paul—the same people his heart ached for. Would they ever accept the truth as he had—that Jesus Christ was the Messiah their own prophets had spoken of?

Looking back over the centuries we cannot see a great awakening to this truth on the part of the Jewish people. Paul would be saddened indeed. However, according to the Scriptures, repentance and salvation will ultimately come to the nation of Israel. In the meantime, the Good News is being spread throughout the world to both Jewish and Gentile people and God's kingdom continues to grow.

CHALLENGE: The Gentile people have been adopted into God's family with the same love and devotion that He has in His heart for the Jewish people.

READ: Acts 3:17-19 – Peter is reminding the Jewish people what their prophets had foretold about the Messiah. Read: Acts 26:22-23 – Paul is also quoting the prophets of old. What common prophecy about the Messiah do we see?

READ: Zechariah 12:10-11, Romans 11:12, 11:25-27 – What do these verses say about the Jewish people in times to come?

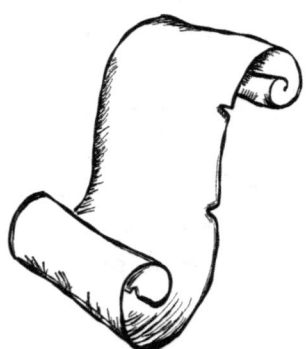

9:6-9 – "Well then, has God failed to fulfill His promise to Israel? No, for not all who are born into the nation of Israel are truly members of God's people! Being descendants of Abraham doesn't make them truly Abraham's children. For the Scriptures say, "Isaac is the son through whom your descendants will be counted," though Abraham had other children, too. This means that Abraham's physical descendants are not necessarily children of God. Only the children of the promise are considered to be Abraham's children. For God had promised, "I will return about this time next year, and Sarah will have a son."

Not all of Abraham's descendants are children of the promise.

God said to Abraham, "Sarah, your wife, will give birth to a son for you. You will name him Isaac, and I will confirm my covenant with him and his descendants as an everlasting covenant." (Gen. 17:19) God's covenant with Abraham was limited to Isaac's line. He was the promised son who Sarah bore in her old age. It would be through his line that the Messiah would be born. (Matt. 1:2, Luke 3:34) It would be through his line that "all the families on earth" would be blessed. (Gen. 12:3b)

Has God kept His promise? Yes, He has!

Through supernatural intervention Isaac was born to Abraham and Sarah. Over thirty generations later, Jesus, the promised Messiah, was born, and *through Him* we can be born again—we can become children of the promise.

The point Paul is making here is to show us that we are not automatically children of God in the same way that not every descendant of Abraham can automatically be counted among the children of the promise. They can only be so *through* Isaac. And we can only become a child of God *through* Jesus Christ.

Charles Spurgeon said, "God's children are not the product of nature, they are not begotten by man, but by Him." It takes God's supernatural intervention for us to become one of His children. It is a redemptive work on His part that only He can accomplish in us so that we can be counted among the children of the promise—God's child.

CHALLENGE: To be a child of God takes more than having the correct DNA. We must have the Son of God within us to be called HIS.

READ: II Samuel 7:12-16 – What other covenant promise did God make within the descendants of Isaac?

READ: Genesis 21:13, Hosea 3:4-5, and Isaiah 11:11-13 – What are we told concerning the rest of Abraham's descendants in times yet to come?

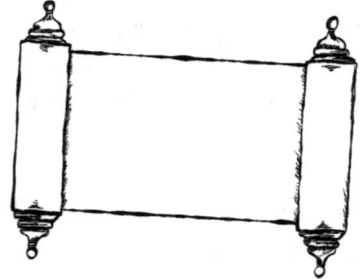

9:9-12 – "For God had promised, 'I will return about this time next year, and Sarah will have a son.' This son was our ancestor Isaac. When he married Rebekah, she gave birth to twins. But before they were born, before they had done anything good or bad, she received a message from God. (This message shows that God chooses people according to His own purposes; He calls people, but not according to their good or bad works.) She was told, 'Your older son will serve your younger son.'"

Who has more right or ability to be in charge of this world than its Creator?

God told Abraham and Sarah they would have a son. Isaac was that son. Then God told Isaac's wife, Rebekah, that she would have twins and the older of the two would serve the younger. We know from Scripture that Jacob and Esau were the twins born and indeed, Jacob, the younger, ended up with the patriarchal blessing. What we see here is God's sovereignty in action—God making choices that fulfill His ultimate plan. As the Creator of all there is, this is His right.

God has a master plan for redeeming mankind—the plan of salvation. We can join Him and be a part of that plan, or not. God will never force us to join Him.

When Jesus asked His disciples if they would remain with Him—be a part of His plan—or leave Him like others had, Peter responded with this statement: "Lord, to whom would we go? You have the words that give eternal life." (John 6:68) Peter knew that without Jesus there is no hope. There is no other plan of salvation.

So again we ask; who has more right and ability to be in charge of this world?

God is love, so we know there is no maliciousness in Him. God is wise, so we know His decisions are made with great discernment. God is just, so we know His decisions are fair. God is righteous, so we know His decisions are right. God is kind and merciful, so we know His decisions are not meant to harm us but are meant for our good. God is faithful, so we know *He can be trusted.*

CHALLENGE: The choice to be a part of God's plan is ours to make. His desire is that none should perish; that all would join Him. (II Peter 3:9)

READ: I Corinthians 8:6 – Explain this verse in your own words.

READ: Deuteronomy 4:39 and II Samuel 7:22 – How do these verses support Peter's answer to Jesus in John 6:68?

9:13 – "In the words of the Scriptures, 'I loved Jacob, but I rejected Esau.'" (Some translations say: "Jacob I loved, but Esau I hated.")

I will always reject a candy bar with no nuts over one with nuts. This doesn't mean I hate candy bars with no nuts. I simply prefer one with nuts.

Hate is a strong word and must be looked at here in its context and culture. The Hebrews used "love" and "hate" as a way of comparison. We see this in Genesis 29:30 in reference to Jacob's relationships with Rachel and Leah. Leah was "loved less" than Rachel by comparison. Not hated.

In many cultures it is the practice for the father to leave his estate to his eldest son. This doesn't mean he hates the younger one. That's just the way it's often done. However, if the oldest son has proven himself to be irresponsible, the father may choose to bypass him and name the younger son his heir. Even in this, it doesn't mean he hates his older son. By choosing one and rejecting the other the father is hoping to do right by all those who come behind. This is his right.

As we saw in Day 63, God has a master plan and He chooses to work it out *His way*. We also understand that He has every right to do so. The Scriptures say: "The heavens are yours, and the earth is yours; everything in the world is yours—you created it all." "The earth is the LORD'S, and everything in it. The world and all its people belong to Him." (Ps. 89:11, Ps. 24:1)

God had the right to choose Jacob over Esau. They both belonged to Him and He had a plan that included both them and their ancestors—a plan that would ultimately lead to the redemption of mankind.

CHALLENGE: We must trust Him with His plan because *He can be trusted.*

READ: Romans 2:11, Acts 10:34, Job 34:19, and Deuteronomy 10:17 – What character quality of God do these verses stress?

READ: Psalm 9:10, and John 13:7 – How can these verses give us hope and help us trust God?

DAY 65

9:14-16 – "Are we saying, then, that God was unfair? Of course not! For God said to Moses, "I will show mercy to anyone I choose, and I will show compassion to anyone I choose." So it is God who decides to show mercy. We can neither choose it nor work for it."

Everything that exists belongs to and is known by its Creator; God.

Mankind would like to take God out of this position, believing that the world is in control of itself from the very beginning to the very end. This kind of thinking is described in Romans 1:21. Mankind knows there is a God; they simply refuse to admit it. They come up with all sorts of foolish ideas about God, attempting to put Him in a box or do away with Him all together. But the truth remains. "Oh God, the heavens are yours, and the earth is yours; everything in the world is yours—you created it all." (Ps. 89:11)

While speaking with Job God said, "Who has given me anything that I need to pay back? Everything under heaven is mine." (Job 41:11) It can't be stated any clearer than that!

If we consider today's verses in view of God exercising His right and authority as Creator/Owner, and knowing Him to be loving, kind, just, wise, and righteous, we can rest assured that "God causes everything to work together for the good of those who love Him (God) and are called according to His purposes for them." (Rom. 8:28)

We can't limit God to the practices or traditions of mankind. When it comes to Jacob and Esau, God simply chose Jacob and rejected Esau for his own reasons and purpose. (Please read Malachi 1:1-5) God had a plan. These two men would be the founders of Israel (Jacob) and Edom (Esau). Israel would become God's chosen people while Edom would become their bitter enemy. (see Amos 1:11)

God knows the heart of each and every one of us, but His plans are not determined by our whims and wishes. He has a plan far greater than we could ever imagine.

To help me understand this, Mom told me to think of it as a parade. As a bystander, I can only see the part of the parade that is currently in front of me. God can see the whole parade!

CHALLENGE: We must leave the parade directing to God!

READ: Ephesians 3:20, and Isaiah 55:8 – Explain the truth these verses are declaring.

READ: Proverbs 16:9 and 19:21 – What truth about God do we see here?

READ: Psalm 33:11 and Isaiah 14:24 – How can these verses give us hope?

DAY 66

9:17-18 – "For the Scriptures say that God told Pharaoh, 'I have appointed you for the very purpose of displaying my power in you and to spread my fame throughout the earth.' So you see, God chooses to show mercy to some and he chooses to harden the hearts of others so they refuse to listen."

No one deserves God's grace and not all will accept it when it is offered.

If we look at the Pharaoh's past record, when it comes to the Hebrew people, we see a lot of hard-heartedness way before the Exodus. We see the Hebrews being forced to be slaves under brutal task masters who show no mercy. (Exodus 1:11-14) When Pharaoh became concerned about the fact that the Hebrew people far outnumbered the Egyptians and feared a "take over", he commanded the mid-wives to kill every Hebrew baby boy at birth to stop their population growth. When that didn't work, he decreed that every Hebrew baby boy was to be thrown into the Nile River. (Exodus 1:15-16, 1:22) God's people suffered great cruelty at the hands of the Pharaoh. (Exodus 3:7) This evidence of hard-hearted evilness had convinced Moses that Pharaoh would never let the Hebrew people leave Egypt. (Exodus 3:19)

Pharaoh's heart was already set against God and his resolve was already set against God's people. God allowed Pharaoh to hold to his chosen course by NOT softening his heart—instead, He set it in stone. We know this resulted in the great plagues and judgment in Egypt that ultimately freed the Hebrew people. God used Pharaoh's hard heart to fulfill His sovereign plan for Israel.

The Scriptures tell us God "calls" us to Himself. (John 6:44) It is God who renews the heart. (Titus 3:5) Acts 16:14 tells the story of Lydia—*a lady who worshipped God*—that she was able to listen to what Paul was saying and ultimately accept it because *"the Lord opened her heart."* However, not all will respond positively to God's grace when it is offered to them.

A good example of this is the story of the wealthy young man who knelt before Jesus and asked how he could inherit eternal life. After Jesus reminded him of the commandments—which he said he had kept from his youth—Jesus brought up the one commandment the young man was still not obeying. He was not willing to share his wealth with the poor. The young man sadly walked away while Jesus looked on with "genuine love for

108

him." (Mark 10:17-22) He chose to stick to his course and say, no thank you, to the grace offered to him.

We each have a choice. God doesn't want to lose any of us; but He will not force us to choose against our will. With "genuine love" He has made a way for us to inherit eternal life. He then draws us to Himself through the Good News of Jesus Christ. How it must break His heart when some sadly walk away.

CHALLENGE: In love God passionately reached out to us and offered LIFE everlasting to all. We must choose to change our course and accept His offer.

READ: Luke 10:16 – When the message of salvation is rejected, who is truly being rejected?

JOHN 1:12 – What does it take to be given the right to become children of God?

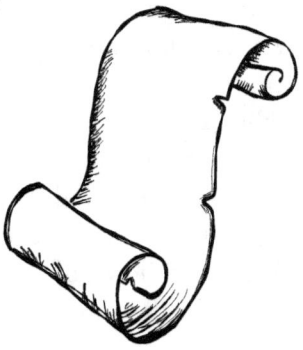

109

DAY 67

9:19-23 – "Well then, you might say, 'Why does God blame people for not responding? Haven't they simply done what He makes them do?' No, don't say that. Who are you, a mere human being, to argue with God? Should the thing that was created say to the one who created it, 'Why have you made me like this?' When a potter makes jars out of clay, doesn't He have a right to use the same lump of clay to make one jar for decorations and another to throw garbage into? In the same way, even though God has the right to show His anger and His power, He is very patient with those on whom His anger falls, who are destined for destruction. He does this to make the riches of His glory shine even brighter on those to whom He shows mercy, who were prepared in advance for Glory."

God has the right to do whatever He wants with whatever He wants and with whomever He wants. He also has the right to exercise this right or to choose not to.

These verses put us firmly in our place and leave us in no doubt that the world *does not spin around us*. God is creator, we are His creation. God is working out His plan for mankind, we can work with Him, or we can work against Him. But we cannot take Him out of the equation as some would like to do—claiming mankind is in control of everything. We must look at the TRUTH.

God created the heavens and the earth—He holds it all together. He created mankind—knowing they would rebel against Him, separating them from Him forever. He then set in motion a most unfathomable plan to bring them back to Him. Instead of angrily exercising His right to condemn this willfully sinful race, *in love* He sent His Son, Jesus, to pay the cost for their sin and unrighteousness, so they could be reunited with Him. The cost of their redemption was not cheap—it took the life of His Son to remove them from His wrath—wrath that was fully justified.

His plan is in place—how each person fits into the plan is up to them. The opportunity to accept or reject the gift of grace and forgiveness is *offered* to ALL, for God is just and fair. But not *all* will accept it. John 1:12 says, "But to all who believed Him and accepted Him, He gave the right to become children of God." To those who *believe* they need to be forgiven by God for their sins against Him, and who desire to accept His offer of

110

forgiveness through the work of Jesus Christ, God makes it possible for them to become His children.

Only God knows each heart. (Acts 15:8) He knows who will or will not choose to be a part of His salvation plan. Those who reject Him are destined for destruction, being condemned because of their sin. However, in John 5:24 Jesus says, "Those who listen to my message and believe in God who sent Me have eternal life. They will never be condemned for their sins, but they have already passed from death into life."

CHALLENGE: The choice is ours. God has chosen to have a family of people to call His own. Are you a member of His family?

READ: II Peter 3:9 – What does this verse tell us about God's heart?

READ: I Peter 1:3-5 – What does God have for those who are "prepared in advance for His glory."?

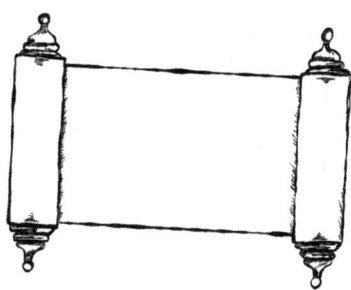

111

DAY 68

9:24-26 – "And we are among those whom He selected, both from the Jews and from the Gentiles. Concerning the Gentiles, God says in the prophecy of Hosea, 'Those who were not my people, I will now call my people. And I will love those whom I did not love before.' And, 'Then, at the place where they were told, 'You are not my people,' there they will be called 'children of the living God.'"

There is one Body of Believers and it is made up of both Jews and Gentiles.

From the beginning God had a plan to gather around Himself a redeemed family that would include both Jews and Gentiles. The Jews, being God's chosen people, had a difficult time understanding and accepting the inclusion of the Gentiles.

Paul uses words from one of Israel's own prophets to support his message concerning the Gentiles. "Those who were not my people, I will now call my people." And "…they will be called 'children of the living God.'" (Hosea 2:22) He makes it clear to his readers that God has personally chosen each of them—both Jew and Gentile—to be a part of His church family. They are to love one another, serve one another, encourage one another, pray for one another, and as brothers and sisters in the Lord, accept one another. For Jesus said, "Your love for one another will prove to the world that you are my disciples." (I Pet. 4:8, Gal. 5:13, Heb. 10:25, James 5:16, Rom. 15:7, John 13:35)

Paul knew that for the church to grow and mature they needed to have unity. They needed to get away from "Jew" or "Gentile" and embrace being "disciples of Jesus Christ".

This is true for the church today. We must stay true to the essentials of God's word and not get caught up in the enemy's trap of having "godless, foolish discussions." (I Tim. 6:20)

We each need to stop focusing on "self" and focus on the ONE we follow and serve.

I personally believe our time is limited—the return of Christ not being so very far away. Jesus said, "We must quickly carry out the tasks assigned us by the One who sent us. The night is coming and then no one can work." (John 9:4)

112

CHALLENGE: The church has a big job to do. It will be more fruitful if we do it together in the Spirit of Jesus Christ.

READ: Acts 13:46 – Why does Paul say the gospel was preached to the Gentiles?

READ: Ephesian 4:1-6 – Record all the "ones" in this passage. How do you think following Paul's instructions in these verses would benefit the church?

DAY 69

9:27-29 – "And concerning Israel, Isaiah the prophet cried out, 'Though the people of Israel are as numerous as the sand of the seashore, only a remnant will be saved. For the Lord will carry out His sentence upon the earth quickly and with finality.' And Isaiah said the same thing in another place; 'If the Lord of Heaven's Armies had not spared a few of our children, we would have been wiped out like Sodom, destroyed like Gomorrah.'"

God has always taken the first step toward mankind.

For centuries the people of Israel took one step forward and two steps back in their faithfulness to God. They preferred to trust in their works to gain righteousness rather than surrendering in obedience to God.

Paul reminds his readers of Isaiah's prophecy concerning Israel. If it wasn't for the grace of God, the whole nation would have been wiped out—condemned! Can you hear the anguish in Isaiah's voice as he tries to warn his people that a day of reckoning is coming and it will be final? However, God will choose to be gracious to His willful people and gather to Himself a remnant to call His own.

Isaiah's words of warning are laced with hope—hope based on God's sovereign choice to perform *a work of grace* that Israel's free will would not choose for itself.

This is the same state that mankind is in today—the same willful heart, the same righteous God offering the same *work of grace*. Each must come to the conclusion that he cannot save himself and by rejecting God's grace he condemns himself.

The Scriptures tell us that mankind doesn't naturally seek out God or salvation. So we must conclude that God's sovereign acts of grace are of greater benefit than mankind's free will. (Romans 3:10-12, 8:7, Ephesians 2:3) By His grace, God spared a remnant of Jews from destruction, and by His grace *He offers* salvation to all who will believe and accept His offer.

CHALLENGE: God always takes the first step toward us. Will we respond by running back to Him?

READ: Romans 11:5 – How did a few Jews remain faithful to God?

READ: John 6:44, 65 – What do these verses tell us about God and mankind?

READ: Psalm 19:1-4 and Romans 1:19-20 – Does God want us to know Him or has He kept Himself a secret from mankind?

READ: II Peter 3:9 and Acts 1:8 – The Good News is the key to salvation. Has God limited the Good News to a few or was His plan to have it spread throughout the world?

DAY 70

9:30-33 – "What does all this mean? Even though the Gentiles were not trying to follow God's standards, they were made right with God. And it was by faith that this took place. But the people of Israel, who tried so hard to get right with God by keeping the law, never succeeded. Why not? Because they were trying to get right with God by keeping the law instead of by trusting in Him. They stumbled over the great rock in their path. God warned them of this in the Scriptures when He said, 'I am placing a stone in Jerusalem that makes people stumble, a rock that makes them fall. But anyone who trusts in Him will never be disgraced.'"

Jesus was the obstacle that kept Israel from being made right with God.

Once again Paul quotes the prophet Isaiah concerning Israel. This time he focuses on their rejection of Jesus as their Messiah—describing Him as a "great rock" that trips them up from being made right with God. (Isaiah 8:14, 28:16) Following the law was what they knew—this was in their history. Putting their faith in the One they had crucified was out of the question.

The Gentiles, however, had no such history. By faith they had embraced the Good News of Jesus Christ and as a result, were being adopted into the family of God.

Israel rejected Jesus' redemptive work on their behalf, choosing instead to cling to the futility of following the law to obtain righteousness. Through the words of Isaiah, their own prophet, Paul tells them they can have peace with God if they would put their faith in the Rock—Jesus Christ.

Mankind still attempts to gain eternal life through "works". Like the people of Israel, they would rather do it themselves. But that's not God's way! Salvation is a free gift of grace given by God. It cannot be earned in any way. No one can then brag about it because no work on our part can contribute to salvation. (Eph. 2:8-9)

Having sins forgiven and being made right with God *by trusting in Jesus Christ* is Good News. But the Jewish people didn't understand it. Nathanael expressed the Jewish mindset best in John 1:46. When he was told by Philip that they had found the One spoken of by Moses and the prophets and his name is Jesus of Nazareth. Nathanael said, "Nazareth! Can anything good come from Nazareth?"

Israel's obstacle was seeing Jesus as an interloper—not as their Messiah.

CHALLENGE: Jesus is the Rock of our salvation. (Psalm 95:1) By trusting in Him we have a spiritual foundation that cannot be shaken

READ: I Peter 2:8 – According to this verse why do people stumble?

READ: I Corinthians 10:4 – How is Jesus described in this verse?

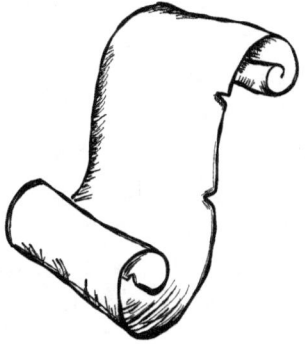

DAY 71

10:1-4 – "Dear brothers and sisters, the longing of my heart and my prayer to God is for the people of Israel to be saved. I know what enthusiasm they have for God, but it is misdirected zeal. For they don't understand God's way of making people right with Himself. Refusing to accept God's way, they cling to their own way of getting right with God by trying to keep the law. For Christ has already accomplished the purpose for which the law was given. As a result, all who believe in Him are made right with God."

Being stuck in our old ways can sometimes lead to stagnation and huge spiritual loss.

Paul is heavily burdened for the salvation of his fellow Israelites. He believes in their genuine commitment to God, but is also aware of their rejection of His Son. They continue to follow the law, seeking righteousness through their works instead of trusting in Jesus.

Like the rest of the Jewish people, Paul knew the law contained the standards and instructions for living in obedience to God—including the instructions for sacrifices that would cover their guilt of sin. However, Paul now knows this "way" is over and a new "way" has come and fulfilled the law through its sinlessness. (Rom.7:6, Gal.5:18)

Jesus was the ultimate sacrifice once and for all. (I Pet.3:18) His Spirit would now dwell within the hearts of His people, and along with His word, would comfort, convict, and instruct them in righteousness. (Ez.36:27) By putting their faith in Jesus, they could be made right with God—they would have eternal life. God knew the Gentiles and many Jews would stumble over this new way.

Change is hard, especially when things have been done a certain way for generations. But the writer of Hebrews says the new way is better. The old system under the Law of Moses was only a shadow of the good things to come. (Heb.9:10-12, 10:1)

Sometimes God has to give us a boost to get us moving in a new direction; this is not always comfortable. But His ways and plans can be trusted to work out in our best interest and for His glory. If God is at work and wanting to make a change in our life, it will be in accordance with Scripture, and His Spirit will guide us step by step. The Lord is completely trustworthy!

CHALLENGE: If we are walking closely with God, we will recognize His voice and leading when the time comes.

READ: Hebrews 10:1-2 – What could the sacrifices NOT do for the people in reference to their relationship with God?

READ: Romans 5:9-11 – How does Christ's death affect our relationship with God?

READ: John 14:26 and John 16:13 – How has the *new way* benefitted believers when it comes to having the Holy Spirit within?

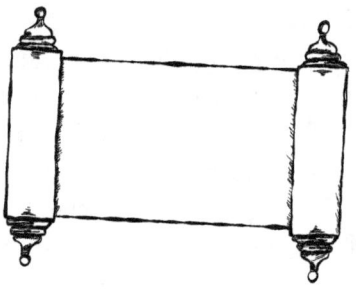

DAY 72

10:5-10 – "For Moses writes that the law's way of making a person right with God requires obedience to all of its commands. But faith's way of getting right with God says, 'Don't say in your heart, 'Who will go up to heaven?' (to bring Christ down to earth). And don't say, 'Who will go down to the place of the dead?' (to bring Christ back to life again).' In fact, it says, 'The message is very close at hand; it is on your lips and in your heart.' And that message is the very message about faith that we preach. If you confess with your mouth that Jesus is Lord and believe in your heart that God raised Him from the dead, you will be saved. For it is by believing in your heart that you are made right with God and it is by confessing with our mouth that you are saved."

One's behavior is not ALWAYS evidence of what's in the heart.

The people of Israel were to obey the law on *all* points. If they broke one part of the law, they were guilty of breaking the whole law. It was *the way* of keeping their behavior/life in line with God's requirements for righteousness. (Lev. 18:4-5, Gal.3:10, James 2:10) But even though the law could motivate them to *act* righteously, it could not *make their hearts* right with God. The Pharisees *acted* righteous, but Jesus called them hypocrites and said they were like whitewashed tombs—beautiful on the outside but filled with dead people's bones and impurity on the inside. (Matt. 23:27) God knows each heart. He knows if the outward behavior matches what is in the heart.

The people of that day were very much like the people of today. It was, and still is, often believed that one can work their way into a right relationship with God. Some believe that by being good, giving money, attending church, or even by attempting to keep the Ten Commandments, God will look favorably on them. But the Scriptures say it is through placing our faith in Jesus Christ that one is made right with God. He gives us His righteousness through faith in Him.

People through the ages have tried to skirt around Jesus—making up their own standards and requirements for salvation. Yet the message is clear. Having a right relationship with God and receiving eternal life is as close as one's lips and heart. That message is: "If you confess with your mouth that Jesus is Lord and believe in your heart that God raised Him from the dead, you will be saved." This is the message Paul preached in Romans 10:9 and the message we still preach today.

Jesus said, "I am the way, the truth, and the life. No one can come to the Father except through me." (John 14:6)

CHALLENGE: We need to stop running away from Jesus Christ but in faith, run to Him.

READ: Jeremiah 17:10 – What does this verse say about our heart and our behavior?

READ: Acts 15: 11 – It takes faith on our part to be saved. What does it take on God's part?

DAY 73

10:11-13 – "As the Scriptures tell us, 'Anyone who trusts in Him will never be disgraced.' Jew or Gentile are the same in this respect. They have the same Lord, who gives generously to all who call on Him. For 'Everyone who calls on the name of the Lord will be saved.'"

There will be one flock with one Shepherd...Jesus Christ!

Trusting in Jesus gives us a foundation that cannot be shaken. He is true and faithful, so He will never blind-side or disappoint us. He is sovereign, so He can never be wrong or mistaken. He does more than we could ever ask or think, so we will never be disillusioned by Him. *Whether Jew or Gentile*, He is the same God and offers the same salvation to anyone who puts their faith in Him.

Paul is quoting Isaiah who said, "Whoever believes need never be shaken." He goes on to quote the prophet Joel who wrote, "Anyone who calls on the name of the Lord will be saved." (Isaiah 28:16, Joel 2:32) God did not keep Jesus or salvation a secret from His people. Throughout the Old Testament He told them through the prophets that a Savior would come. They knew about and expected a Messiah. What they didn't get was that the Gentiles would also be rescued by *their* Messiah. This is one stumbling stone that has given them a hard time believing Jesus is who He said He was. Being a Jew himself, Paul understood their resistance and continued speaking the Good News of Jesus Christ to them.

Jesus said in John 10:16, "I have other sheep, too, that are not in this sheepfold. I must bring them also. They will listen to my voice, and there will be one flock with one shepherd."

CHALLENGE: We are all saved the same way—through faith in Jesus—and we are all loved and cared for by the same Father God.

READ: I Timothy 4:10 – Paul speaks here of his suffering and struggles in ministry. He then makes his mission statement. What is it?

READ: John 3:36 – This is the gospel stated clearly and simply. Is anyone excluded from having the opportunity to be saved?

READ: Isaiah 50:7 – Isaiah makes a familiar statement here. What is it and how does it motivate him in his life?

10:14-17 – "But how can they call on Him to save them unless they believe in Him? And how can they believe in Him if they have never heard about Him? And how can they hear about Him unless someone tells them? And how will anyone go and tell them without being sent? That is why the Scriptures say, 'How beautiful are the feet of messengers who bring good news!' But not everyone welcomes the Good News, for Isaiah the prophet said, 'Lord, who has believed our message?' So faith comes from hearing, that is, hearing the Good News about Christ."

The more we know about something the more likely we are to believe it.

This portion of Scripture is very direct and practical. Before we can believe something, we must know about it; therefore, we must hear or learn about it from someone or some source.

Paul is stressing the importance of evangelism. Before someone can be saved, they have to know they are lost, then they will be open to hearing the way of salvation—the Good News.

As the Gospel is shared, seeds of faith are planted in the heart of the one who hears. As that faith begins to grow, the door of belief opens and the hearer's response is to call upon the name of the Lord. And "everyone who calls on the name of the Lord will be saved." (Acts 2:21)

Messengers are needed so the Gospel can be heard, and the call is not just for full-time missionaries. The apostle Peter said we all need to be ready to explain the hope we have in Christ Jesus. (I Peter 3:15b) Jesus said we are all to go and make disciples in every nation. (Mt.28:19-20)

Unfortunately, not all hearers will believe and accept the truth of Jesus Christ. During His earthly ministry Jesus often experienced rejection. Even His own brothers didn't believe in Him until after His resurrection, but He continued teaching and sharing with all who would hear. (John 7:5)

Salvation is the work of God but we are called to be His witnesses. In a similar way, God said to Ezekiel, "You must give them my message whether they listen or not." (Ezekiel 2:7a)

CHALLENGE: We cannot know who will or will not hear. Therefore, we must faithfully share the Good News and leave the rest to God.

READ: Mark 9:23-24 - The father in this story had both faith and unbelief in his heart. Have you ever experienced this type of dilemma? Did you ask God for help like this father did?

READ: Luke 9:51-56 – Did Jesus let rejection stop Him from doing what He needed to do?

READ: John 17:3 – What does this verse say concerning eternal life and God?

11:1-6 – "I ask, then, has God rejected his own people, the nation of Israel? Of course not! I myself am an Israelite, a descendant of Abraham and a member of the tribe of Benjamin. No, God has not rejected His own people, whom He chose from the very beginning. Do you realize what the Scriptures say about this? Elijah the prophet complained to God about the people of Israel and said, 'Lord, they have killed your prophets and torn down your altars. I am the only one left, and now they are trying to kill me, too.' And do you remember God's reply? He said, 'No, I have 7,000 others who have never bowed down to Baal!' It is the same today, for a few of the people of Israel have remained faithful because of God's grace—His underserved kindness in choosing them. And since it is through God's kindness, then it is not by their good works. For in that case, God's grace would not be what it really is—free and undeserved."

God's faithfulness to His people is evidence of who He is.

God has not and will not reject or abandon His people. He said, "I am as likely to reject my people Israel as I am to abolish the laws of Nature!" (Jer. 31:36)

Israel rebelled against God over and over, while He over and over forgave them. They knew God and they knew the mighty acts He had performed on their behalf—the stories had been passed down through the generations. Yet they continued to run after other gods. A thread of sin and rebellion wove its way through the nation, keeping them from accepting God as their only true god and later Jesus as their Messiah.

Elijah and the other prophets experienced this rejection as they relayed to the people God's pleas and warnings. Yet the Jews refused to listen. But not every heart was hard to Him. There has always been a remnant of faithful followers within the people of Israel. God has chosen them as seed for future generations to ensure a remnant remains. (Isaiah 11:12, 28:5)

Israel cannot claim any part in God's faithfulness to them, just as believers cannot claim any part in their salvation. It is ALL accomplished by God's grace. It is His character to extend grace and forgiveness; it is His character to be faithful. He cannot deny who He is. (II Tim. 2:13)

We are loved because HE is love – I John 4:8

We are forgiven because HE paid the fine – I Peter 2:24, Colossians 1:13-14

We are His children because HE made it possible – John 1:12

We have eternal life because HE gave us His Spirit through His Son – Titus 3:5-7

This God is our GOD!

CHALLENGE: God's example of faithfulness should guide our hearts and behavior toward faithfulness.

READ: II Timothy 2:13 – What happens when we are unfaithful?

ACCORDING TO ROM. 11:1 how does Paul support the truth that God has not rejected Israel?

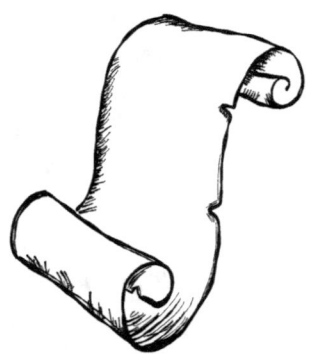

11:7-10 – "So this is the situation: Most of the people of Israel have not found the favor of God they are looking for so earnestly. A few have—the ones God has chosen—but the hearts of the rest were hardened. As the Scriptures say, 'God has put them into a deep sleep. To this day He has shut their eyes so they do not see, and closed their ears so they do not hear.' Likewise, David said, 'Let their bountiful table become a snare, a trap that makes them think all is well. Let their blessings cause them to stumble, and let them get what they deserve. Let their eyes go blind so they cannot see, and let their backs be bent forever.'"

Doing things God's way leads to life—doing things our way leads to death.

The truth of that statement is evident throughout the Scriptures; especially when it comes to the nation of Israel. They continually tried to be made right with God through the works of the law. But the law could not make them righteous. When Jesus came and the new covenant was introduced to them, most rejected it. They would not accept the fact that righteousness comes through faith in Jesus Christ, not through the law.

Some believed and embraced the Truth, but most would remain blind and deaf to this new way. They saw it as a ploy to draw them away from what they knew and understood. They were comfortable in their traditions and content doing things the old way. They wanted no part of Jesus, who claimed to be the One spoken of by the prophets. They couldn't see that their contentment kept them from belief in the risen Savior.

God never forces anyone to believe. The invitation is given to all and it is the responsibility of each individual to respond to it. If the invitation is rejected, the individual will receive the consequences God has planned for unbelievers—death—separation from God in hell. If it is received, the believer will be given eternal life with Him in heaven.

As a nation, Israel has not embraced the opportunity of having a personal relationship with God through Christ Jesus. However, they will one day have their eyes opened and they will finally accept the Truth. (Rom. 11:25)

CHALLENGE: We each must choose by faith to accept Christ…this is God's way!

READ: Isaiah 35:4-5,10 and Zechariah 12:10-11 – What do these verses tell us about Israel's future?

READ: Luke 7:28-30 – How did the Jewish religious leaders respond to God's plan for them?

READ: John 5:24, 47 – How does one pass from death into life?

11:11-12 – "Did God's people stumble and fall beyond recovery? Of course not! They were disobedient, so God made salvation available to the Gentiles. But He wanted His own people to become jealous and claim it for themselves. Now if the Gentiles were enriched because the people of Israel turned down God's offer of salvation, think how much greater a blessing the world will share when they finally accept it."

There is no *quit* in God's mercy and grace.

The Jewish people rejected God's offer of salvation so He extended His invitation to the Gentiles. He was not rejecting Israel in doing this, He was just allowing His grace and mercy to overflow to the Gentiles. God cannot and will not deny Himself the joy of being "Lord God" to lost people who have no hope without Him—whether Jew or Gentile. (Neh. 9:17-18)

Grace—giving what is not deserved, and *mercy*—withholding what is rightly deserved, come from a heart that doesn't know how to NOT be gracious and merciful to all who would call on Him.

These two elements of God's character make it possible for us to be forgiven of our sin and its consequences and to have a personal relationship with Him forever. This is the Good News of salvation, brought about through God's grace and mercy. (Eph. 2:8, Col. 2:13)

When the people of Israel rejected God's gracious offer, He mercifully extended that offer to the Gentiles in an attempt to stir the Jews to jealousy. One day they will return to the Lord their God, but in the meantime the Gentiles are benefiting from the Jewish rebellion. God's eternal kingdom and family is multiplying and when the Jews once again turn to Him. The reunion will be a wondrous thing to behold. We know at least 144,000 from the twelve tribes of Israel will be a part of this reunion. What a time that will be!! (Rev. 7:4, Zech. 12:10)

CHALLENGE: Without God's grace and mercy mankind would be hopeless. Our calling as followers of Jesus Christ is to tell others about the hope we have in Him. (I Pet. 3:15)

READ: Jeremiah 31:36 – Explain the meaning of this verse in context with today's study.

READ: Isaiah 43:25 and Psalm 103:12 – What does God do with our sin according to these verses?

READ: I John 1:9 – What happens when we confess our sins to God?

11:13-16 – "I am saying all this especially for you Gentiles. God has appointed me as the apostle to the Gentiles. I stress this for I want somehow to make the people of Israel jealous of what you Gentiles have, so I might save some of them. For since their rejection meant that God offered salvation to the rest of the world, their acceptance will be even more wonderful. It will be life for those who were dead! And since Abraham and the other patriarchs were holy, their descendants will also be holy—just as the entire batch of dough is holy because the portion given as an offering is holy. For if the roots of the tree are holy, the branches will be, too."

God has a plan!!!

Paul's desire to see salvation come to his people had not been dampened by their rejection of Jesus. He knew God has not given up on Israel, for they are deeply rooted in His heart, along with the holy patriarchs whose bloodline produced the Messiah. Paul also knows that Israel's rejection of Jesus opened the way of salvation for the Gentiles. As they come to accept the Good News and put their faith in Jesus Christ. His desire is that the Jews will become jealous of the Gentile's new relationship with *their* God and the hope they are finding in His Son.

Paul believes this stirring to jealousy will bring life to the children of Israel, who now are spiritually dead. The Kingdom of God would grow to His honor and glory, being built up with both Jewish and Gentile believers who are following the Holy One—Jesus the Messiah.

We know this did not happen with Israel *as a nation*. However, many Jews did become believers, and today Jews are accepting Jesus Christ. One day the nation of Israel will have their eyes opened and they will come to know their Messiah—they will become followers of Jesus *as a nation*.

As Christians, we share Christ's life—His Spirit. We wear His righteousness and have the honor of calling God, "Abba Father". (Rom. 8:15) The whole world has been offered this opportunity because Israel said *no* to Jesus: at Calvary. (John 3:16)

God has a plan and we must trust Him as He works it out. Knowing we are part of the plan should keep us diligent in our spiritual growth and kingdom service.

CHALLENGE: The ability to rest in God's sovereign plan comes from having an intimate knowledge of Him.

READ: Isaiah 37:32 – What does this verse tell us about God's relationship with His people Israel?

READ: Ephesians 1:5 - Explain this verse and how it fits into today's lesson.

READ: Zechariah 12:10 – This verse speaks of Israel mourning. What are they mourning over?

11:17-20 – "But some of these branches from Abraham's tree—some of the people of Israel—have been broken off. And you Gentiles, who were branches from a wild olive tree, have been grafted in. So now you also receive the blessing God has promised Abraham and his children, sharing in the rich nourishment from the root of God's special olive tree. But you must not brag about being grafted in to replace the branches that were broken off. You are just a branch, not the root. 'Well,' you may say, 'those branches were broken off to make room for me.' Yes, but remember—those branches were broken off because they didn't believe in Christ, and you are there because you do believe. So don't think highly of yourself, but fear what could happen. For if God did not spare the original branches, He won't spare you either."

The Jew's loss was the Gentile's gain.

From the beginning Israel lived under God's promise and protection. God told Abraham He would make him the father of many nations and He would be their God. (Gen. 17:3-7) Through the prophets He promised them a Savior—a Messiah. He told them where He would be born, (Micah 5:2) from what Jewish line He would descend, (II Sam. 7:12-13) and that His mother would be a virgin. (Is. 7:14) They were told He would speak in parables and perform great miracles. (Is. 35:5-6) They were even told of one who would go before Him to prepare the way—speaking of John the Baptist. (Is. 40:3-4) How then did they not recognize Jesus as their Messiah?

The Scriptures tell us that as Jesus taught in the synagogue the people were amazed because He spoke with real authority—unlike the teachers of religious law. (Mark 1:21-22) Perhaps some even wondered if this teacher could be the Messiah—something the religious leaders would object to in fear of losing their power and authority. In spite of these musings, the Jews rejected Jesus as the Christ, prophesy was fulfilled, and the Gentiles were offered a share in God's promised blessing. (Is. 53:1-3)

Unbelieving Jews were cut off and believing Gentiles were grafted in *by God's grace*. Believing in Jesus Christ as Savior and Lord is still the "way" of being made right with God and becoming part of His family.

CHALLENGE: Whether Jew or Gentile, it is by *God's grace* that we are saved—we have nothing to boast about in it. (Eph. 2:8-9)

READ: I Corinthians 10:12 – How does this verse fit in with today's thinking?

READ: Jeremiah 51:5 and Leviticus 26:44-45 – Has God forsaken Israel? Explain these verses.

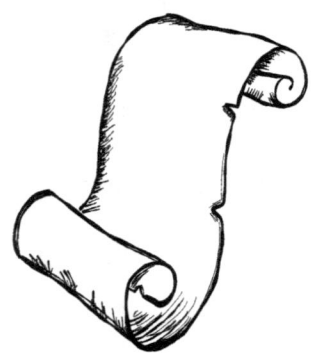

11:19-24 – "'Well,' you may say, 'those branches were broken off to make room for me.' Yes, but remember—those branches were broken off because they didn't believe in Christ, and you are there because you do believe. So don't think highly of yourself, but fear what could happen. For if God did not spare the original branches, he won't spare you either. Notice how God is both kind and severe. He is severe toward those who disobeyed, but kind to you if you continue to trust in His kindness. But if you stop trusting you also will be cut off. And if the people of Israel turn from their unbelief, they will be grafted in again, for God has the power to graft them back into the tree. You, by nature, were a branch cut from a wild olive tree. So if God was willing to do something contrary to nature by grafting you into His cultivated tree, He will be far more eager to graft the original branches back into the tree where they belong."

Belief in Jesus Christ is essential for being in the family of God.

God cut off the Jews because they didn't believe in His Son. They didn't believe He fulfilled the words spoken by the prophets concerning the Messiah, and they didn't believe what Jesus said about Himself. So, in their place, He grafted in the Gentiles who *did* believe and by faith accepted Jesus. God was both just and kind in doing this. He rewarded the Gentiles belief and judged Israel's unbelief.

However, if the Gentiles were to turn away from their belief and the Jews were to believe in Jesus, God would once again graft in the Jews and cut off the Gentiles. Only God has the power to do so—and God has not changed the way He deals with belief and unbelief. He rewards belief in His Son with eternal life. Unbelief brings death and destruction.

In this passage of Scripture, we can see how very important it is to God that we believe in His one and only Son. Jesus IS the Good News. He IS the way, the truth, and the life. Without Him there is no hope—no chance of having a relationship with God.

Jesus was a Jew—a member of the nation of Israel. God chose these people to be His Son's earthly family. Imagine how happy He would be to have them turn in belief to Jesus Christ.

CHALLENGE: God's family is made up of ALL who believe in Jesus Christ. He is the Root that connects us to God—our Father.

READ: I John 5:11-13 – What has God made plain to us through this passage?

READ: Acts 4:12 – What does this verse tell us about salvation?

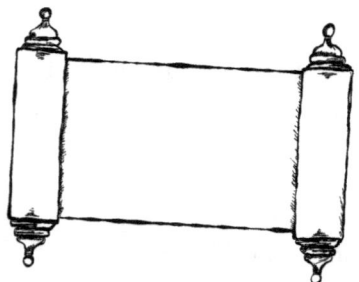

DAY 81

11:25-27 – I want you to understand this mystery, dear brothers and sisters, so that you will not feel proud about yourselves. Some of the people of Israel have hard hearts, but this will last only until the full number of Gentiles comes to Christ. And so all Israel will be saved. As the Scriptures say, 'The one who rescues will come from Jerusalem, and He will turn Israel away from ungodliness. And this is my covenant with them, that I will take away their sins.'"

People like a good mystery.

The mystery revealed in this passage promises hope to the nation of Israel. Their rejection of Jesus cost them the opportunity *as a nation* to open their heart to the new covenant, which is through the very One they crucified. But one day, after the last chosen Gentile is saved, God will soften the nation's heart and they will finally understand that Jesus is the way to righteousness. As with the Gentiles, not all will accept the Gospel, but *as a nation*, all will be given the opportunity.

Paul quotes the prophet Isaiah to support God's sovereign plan to turn Israel from ungodliness and have their sins forgiven through His Son. (Isaiah 59:20-21) This was a mystery because Israel did not accept Jesus as their Messiah. However, Paul wants his readers to understand that there is hope for the nation of Israel. And the mystery is being revealed to keep Gentiles from becoming proud. The Good News was offered to them *because of* Israel's fall.

And one day, Israel will once again be given the opportunity to accept Jesus Christ as their Savior.

Today, God is building His kingdom. It is made up of believing Gentiles *and* Jews who have chosen to put their faith in Jesus Christ. Because only some of the nation has hardened hearts, we must pray for and witness to the Jewish people. Some will accept the Good News.

CHALLENGE: God works everything together for good and according to His sovereign plan. (Romans 8:28)

READ: Jeremiah 13:15-16 – How do these verses fit in with today's verses?

137

READ: Jeremiah 31:16-17 – How do these verses fit in with today's verses?

READ: Zechariah 12:10-14 – What promise do we see concerning Israel?

P.S. CHALLENGE: God's word is amazing and can be trusted to be true!

11:28-33 – "Many of the people of Israel are now enemies of the Good News, and this benefits you Gentiles. Yet they are still the people He loves because He chose their ancestors Abraham, Isaac, and Jacob. For God's gifts and His call can never be withdrawn. Once, you Gentiles were rebels against God, but when the people of Israel rebelled against Him, God was merciful to you instead. Now they are the rebels, and God's mercy has come to you so that they, too, will share in God's mercy. For God has imprisoned everyone in disobedience so He could have mercy on everyone. Oh, how great are God's riches and wisdom and knowledge! How impossible it is for us to understand His decisions and His ways!"

God takes every opportunity to show us His mercy.

God's love for the nation of Israel is deeply rooted in the covenant He made with their forefathers, Abraham, Isaac, and Jacob. Even though He has temporarily set them aside and turned His attention to rescuing the Gentiles, His love for Israel has not changed. God is faithful—He never repents of or takes away from His sovereign plan.

He once showered the Jewish people with mercy, but they rejected Him. He moved on with His plan for mankind by showing mercy to the Gentiles—who now have access to God through His Son and can be heirs of an eternal inheritance. But one day—in His mercy—His focus will return to Israel and He will give them another chance. This time, they will come to recognize and accept Him as their GOD. (Jeremiah 24:7)

I have heard some ask, "If God knew mankind was going to sin, why did He create them?" We see the answer in this passage; so He could have mercy on everyone.

We can't understand why some things happen the way they do. We question God when we experience injustice, disappointment, heartache or pain. But God takes these opportunities to show us His mercy. If we choose to surrender all to Him and rest in His wisdom, knowledge, and promises, we will experience His mercy and peace.

CHALLENGE: Let God shower you with mercy by casting your cares and heavy burdens on Him.

READ: Isaiah 27:6 and Hebrews 8:8-12 – What do these verses tell us about Israel's future?

READ: Psalm 51:1 and Psalm 28:6 – What example concerning mercy can we learn from David?

READ: Lamentations 3:22-23 – What do these verses tell us about God's mercy?

11:34-36 – "For who can know the LORD's thoughts? Who knows enough to give Him advice? And who has given Him so much that He needs to pay it back? For everything comes from Him and exists by His power and is intended for His glory. All glory to Him forever! Amen."

Believing what the Scriptures proclaim about God will produce humility.

Mankind has always been plagued with pride. It began when Satan said, "I will climb to the highest heavens and *be like the Most High*." (Is. 14:13-14 emphasis mine) His prideful deceit continued when he told Eve that if she ate the forbidden fruit, she would "*be like God*" and "the woman was convinced. (Gen. 3:5-6) The rest is history.

With each passing century and with each new invention or idea pride has continued to flourish. God—the creator of it all—has become insignificant in the mind of mankind, who has traded the truth about God for a lie. (Rom. 1:25)

In today's passage, Paul is led by the Holy Spirit to ask his readers the same questions God told Isaiah to ask the Israelites—and that God, Himself asked Job. (Is. 40:13, Job 41:11) Then He answered them for us when He told Isaiah, "My thoughts are nothing like your thoughts" and "my ways are far beyond anything you could imagine." (Is. 55:8-9)

EVERYTHING comes from God, and by HIS POWER everything exists, and it is all intended for His glory. It is there to point us to God—to recognize that He is not only the Creator of all things, but that He is at work in the world and in each individual life, orchestrating His sovereign plan. He IS the Alpha and Omega, the First and the Last, the Beginning and the End. (Rev. 22:13)

CHALLENGE: If we put God in His rightful place, we will be in our rightful place.

READ: Philippians 2:9-11 – One day mankind's pride will be a thing of the past. Use these verses to explain how and why.

READ: Psalm 67:2-4 – Where do we see the purpose for the Church in these verses?

READ: Isaiah 42:8-9 – God speaks of Himself in these verses. What evidence does He give for His right to be glorified? How does that give the believer hope?

DAY 84

12:1 – "And so, dear brothers and sisters, I plead with you to give your bodies to God because of all He has done for you. Let them be a living and holy sacrifice—the kind He will find acceptable. This is truly the way to worship Him."

Dwelling on all God has done for us will have a motivating effect on our service for Him.

Jesus gave His life for us—His blood paid the penalty for our sin. He took on our guilt so we could be free from guilt. We were dead in sin—He made us alive through His resurrected life. Choosing to surrender our life back to Him—with our heart and will in line with His—is true worship. We become His ambassadors.

God said, "Be holy for I am holy." (Lev. 20:26) He wants us to resemble Him—making us acceptable vessels for His service. Others will then give praise to God as they see His life being lived out through us. (Matt. 5:16)

Paul pleads with his readers both then and now to use our lives to honor Christ and in our service for Him. We live in a world that has no hope. Apart from God, all are lost and living without the gift of eternal life as their inheritance. They need the Lord Jesus, but in most cases they don't know it.

As Christ's followers, our responsibility is to make Him known to the world. The Apostles turned the whole world upside down for the name of Christ. (Acts 17:6) We can do the same.

CHALLENGE: There is no greater privilege then representing Jesus Christ. Let us do it well.

READ: II Corinthians 5:20 – What is our job as ambassadors of Jesus Christ?

READ: Romans 1:1 and II Peter 1:1 – How did Peter and Paul see themselves? Explain how they lived this out?

12:2 – "Don't copy the behavior and customs of this world, but let God transform you into a new person by changing the way you think. Then you will learn to know God's will for you, which is good and pleasing and perfect."

We are always growing and changing. Doing so in God's direction is the key to His perfect will.

Becoming more like Christ is God's will for us. We learned in Romans 8:29 that He chose us so we could become like His Son. He faithfully works in our lives teaching, molding, and creating for Himself one who resembles Christ Jesus. (II Cor. 3:18) At the root of this transformation is our salvation which is when the Spirit of God comes to live within us. He is the power needed for our sanctification. We cannot become like Christ apart from Him—all attempts will fall short. We need a complete overhaul—beginning with the way we think.

David told his son Solomon, that he needed to *know God* intimately and worship Him wholeheartedly with a "willing mind." (I Chron. 28:9) Knowing God intimately is a mind changer.

As we grow in our knowledge of God, we naturally take on His likeness and character. We were created in His image, and being *like Him* results from knowing *what He is like*. Paul tells us in Philippians 2:5 that we are to have "the same attitude that Christ Jesus had." We must think like Jesus. To do so, we must first know *how* He thinks. By studying His Word, we can know His mind and His heart—we come to see things through His eyes.

With this knowledge comes the awareness of the sinful world around us and the need for our life to magnify Him. God's will for us is to be so much like His Son that others will see His love, His goodness, His faithfulness, His truth, and His righteousness in us and be drawn to have a relationship with Him as well.

CHALLENGE: Without a transformed mind we cannot see or understand God's good, pleasing, and perfect will.

READ: Ephesians 4:23-24 – Who has the ability to renew our thoughts and attitudes? How were we created to be?

READ: Philippians 4:8 – Explain how this verse can help us in the way we think.

DAY 86

12:3-8 – "Because of the privilege and authority God has given me, I give each of you this warning: Don't think you are better than you really are. Be honest in your evaluation of yourselves, measuring yourselves by the faith God has given us. Just as our bodies have many parts and each part has a special function, so it is with Christ's body. We are many parts of one body, and we all belong to each other. In His grace, God has given us different gifts for doing certain things well. So if God has given you the ability to prophesy, speak out with as much faith as God has given you. If your gift is serving others, serve them well. If you are a teacher, teach well. If your gift is to encourage others, be encouraging. If it is giving, give generously. If God has given you leadership ability, take the responsibility seriously. And if you have a gift for showing kindness to others, do it gladly."

There's no place for pride in the family of God.

In verse three we see three words that should guide our hearts and keep our attitudes in check—"God has given." Once again it is God's grace being poured out on His beloved people. It is nothing we have done or will do that has motivated God to bestow such glorious gifts on His children, it is His sovereign grace.

Through the work of His Holy Spirit He has given to each one gifts to be used within the church body. All the gifts are equally important and necessary for the spiritual health and edification of the church. Like Paul, it is our privilege and responsibility to use our gifts to serve others.

Paul warns us not to get an inflated attitude concerning any gift we may have, for it takes all the gifts working together to complete the task of bringing each member to spiritual maturity. Managing our gifts *well* is the challenge given. They must be used with humility, in unity, and with gladness—serving one another wholeheartedly for the glory of God.

CHALLENGE: Our spiritual gifts can bring us joy as well when used as they are intended—for the edification of each other.

READ: I Corinthians 12:4-7 – List several insights found in these verses concerning spiritual gifts.

READ: I Corinthians 12:11 – Who is in charge of spiritual gifts?

READ: I Peter 4:10-11 – What results from believers using their spiritual gifts well?

144

DAY 87

12:9-12 – "Don't just pretend to love others. Really love them. Hate what is wrong. Hold tightly to what is good. Love each other with genuine affection, and take delight in honoring each other. Never be lazy, but work hard and serve the Lord enthusiastically. Rejoice in our confident hope. Be patient in trouble, and keep on praying."

Giving honor to others doesn't come naturally. That's why supernatural help is needed.

Our culture is so taken up with "I" and "me" that nothing is left for "others" and "one another". This should not be the case, especially within the body of Christ. But the old nature makes for a battle ground wherever we are. We may find it easy to honor the pastor or other church leaders within the body, but how about the Christmas program director that gets all the credit after we spent hours preparing the back drops? That may be more difficult.

However, we are not given exceptions. We are told by God to honestly love and honor one another, steering away from pretense—another characteristic of the world we live in. Being genuine in our love is good in God's eyes and we are to hold to it and work hard at it. After all, we are all on the same team and serve the same Lord—Jesus Christ.

Therefore, let us eagerly serve Him and each other in love so the world will know we belong to Him. This is the kind of love the world will recognize as not only being different, but something to be desired—opening the door for sharing the hope we have in Christ Jesus.

Being a follower of Jesus is not always easy, especially during tough times or when it goes against our human nature. Paul reminds us that in these times we must keep praying. Staying in close communication with the Lord of love will allow His love to flow through us and extend to others. Jesus said, "Your love for one another will prove to the world that you are my disciples." (John 13:35)

CHALLENGE: Giving God *His* proper place of honor in our life will make it easier to honor one another.

READ: Philippians 2:4-5 – We must have the same attitudes Christ had. What characteristics of Christ do we see in these verses and in what ways did we see them lived out in Him?

145

READ: Hebrews 13:1 – How are we to love one another? Why would God use this relationship as the example for the kind of love He wants believers to have for one another?

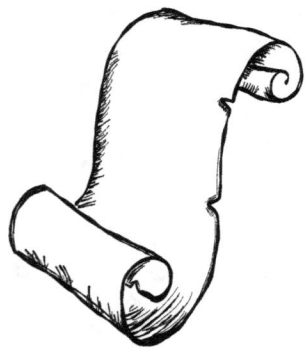

12:13-21 – "When God's people are in need, be ready to help them. Always be eager to practice hospitality. Bless those who persecute you. Don't curse them; pray that God will bless them. Be happy with those who are happy, and weep with those who weep. Live in harmony with each other. Don't be too proud to enjoy the company of ordinary people. And don't think you know it all! Never pay back evil with more evil. Do things in such a way that everyone can see you are honorable. Do all that you can to live in peace with everyone. Dear friends, never take revenge. Leave that to the righteous anger of God.. For the Scriptures say, 'I will take revenge; I will pay them back,' says the Lord. Instead, 'If your enemies are hungry, feed them. If they are thirsty, give them something to drink. In doing this, you will heap burning coals of shame on their heads.' Don't let evil conquer you, but conquer evil by doing good."

As "Christians" we wear the name of Christ.

These verses describe people who are different from those of the world—we who call ourselves "Christian" because we are followers of and devoted to Jesus Christ. It is His character and behavior described in this passage that we are to imitate.

Led by the Spirit, Paul said that we are to be hospitable and sympathetic, and to help those who are in need. In John 6 Jesus was speaking to a crowd of over five thousand people at mealtime. The people became hungry and He saw their need, so He miraculously fed them all. Like Jesus, we are to be driven by compassion and sympathy for others.

Next, we are encouraged to pray for those who mistreat us. In Luke 23:34 Jesus passionately pleaded with His Father to forgive those who were killing Him. Revenge was never something He considered. This kind of love and forgiveness is not *natural* for us and calls for *supernatural* intervention by the Holy Spirit. We are also told to live in harmony with one another. In John 17:11-21 Jesus asked His Father to help His people be united. He wanted us to be of the same heart and mind. However, we are not to be so segregated from the world that we exclude those who need to hear the Good News. Jesus regularly visited and ate with people who needed to know Him—those who were considered by some to be unworthy. (Luke 19:5-7, Matt. 9:10-13) He is our perfect example.

By imitating Jesus, we will have a good and honorable reputation before others. In John 5:19 Jesus said He always does exactly what His

Father does; we are to do the same. This shows to others that we belong to God. For example: Being good to someone who is treating us badly may not come *naturally* to us, but it will shame the offender. Seeing *supernatural,* loving behavior in us can stir their heart and cause them to seek the Lord Jesus.

Paul ends this chapter with a challenge: Keep evil from taking over your life by *choosing* to let *good* control you. God has not left His followers alone to fight our own battles. His Holy Spirit is within us to help us behave *supernaturally* in *naturally* difficult circumstances of life.

CHALLENGE: We must allow God to do His work *in* us, *through* us, and *around* us.

READ: Acts 16:22-25 – Paul and Silas did something supernatural in a naturally difficult situation. What was it?

13:3-5 – "For the authorities do not strike fear in people who are doing right, but in those who are doing wrong. Would you like to live without fear of the authorities? Do what is right and they will honor you. The authorities are God's servants, sent for your good. But if you are doing wrong, of course you should be afraid, for they have the power to punish you. They are God's servants, sent for the very purpose of punishing those who do what is wrong. So you must submit to them not only to avoid punishment, but also to keep a clear conscience."

If we are obeying the traffic laws, we won't panic when we pass an officer of the law.

This passage is very clear. Obey the authorities and we don't have to worry about getting into trouble. It's their God-given job to police those they are responsible for, and it's our job to obey the laws they set forth. God ordained this system for our good.

It's relatively simple and makes good sense; but let's look at the last phrase of today's passage: "Keep a clear conscience." James 4:17 says: "Remember, it is sin to know what you ought to do and then not do it." Known sin always leads to a guilty conscience, but as the Holy Spirit convicts us and stirs our heart to repentance, God offers us I John 1:9. "But if we confess our sins to Him, He is faithful and just to forgive us our sins and to cleanse us from all wickedness."

Confessing our sin tells God that we know we've done wrong and deserve His *displeasure*. Being forgiven restores the peace and joy of knowing God is once again *pleased* with us. King David said it like this: "Restore to me the joy of your salvation, and make me willing to obey you." (Psalm 51:12) Sin had interrupted the joy David had found in his relationship with God. He wanted it back and knew it would come through repentance and obedience to the Lord.

Being afraid of authority when we do wrong should remind us that we are to fear God as well. This is the part we often tend to skirt around. We like to focus on His love and grace and steer clear of His righteous judgment. We can't do that! God has made the way for us to be righteous *before* Him and to keep a close relationship *with* Him. It's our responsibility to be alert to the Spirit's prompting and quickly go to the Savior for forgiveness when we have sinned. A clear conscience is a lot easier to live with then a guilty one. And it's a lot easier to obey our authorities when we first make it our practice to be obedient to God.

CHALLENGE: Freedom from fear and guilt is the reward for obedience.

READ: Acts 5:29 and Luke 20:25 – Explain these verses.

READ: Daniel 3:4-12 – How does this passage support the above verses?

13:6-10 – "Pay your taxes, too, for these same reasons. For government workers need to be paid. They are serving God in what they do. Give to everyone what you owe them: Pay your taxes and government fees to those who collect them, and give respect and honor to those who are in authority. Owe nothing to anyone—except for your obligation to love one another. If you love your neighbor, you will fulfill the requirements of God's law. For the commandments say, 'You must not commit adultery. You must not murder. You must not steal. You must not covet.' These—and other such commandments—are summed up in this one commandment. 'Love your neighbor as yourself.' Love does no wrong to others, so love fulfills the requirements of God's law."

We can try to follow all 613 commandments in the Old Testament law, or we can go to the heart of the law and love our neighbor as our self.

This passage says it shows respect and honor to our authorities by paying what we owe; whether it's our taxes or any other kind of debt. But it goes much deeper than the legality of not being delinquent; it goes straight to the heart. We must be motivated to do so with integrity and a heart that has a love for others—for if we love as Jesus loved, we will naturally do what is right and fair.

When we are motivated by love, we will do to others as we would like them to do to us. (Lk. 6:31) We will live a moral life, respecting the life and property of others—being content with what God has given to us. Love will keep us from doing wrong to others and will stir us to have as much concern for those around us as we do for ourselves.

One day Jesus met a rich man who wanted more—he wanted eternal life. After Jesus quoted some commandments from the law, he got excited. He had kept all these from his youth! However, when Jesus told him to do something that required having love for others, he went away sad—which in turn, made Jesus sad. (Mark 10:17-22)

According to today's passage, having Christ-like love for others will manifest itself in our behavior and attitude toward all those around us. This pleases God because it imitates His heart; which He made known to us through the law.

CHALLENGE: Showing love for others will allow them to see the heart of God through us.

READ: Mark 6:34, Matthew 14:14 and 15:32 – What do these verses have in common concerning Jesus?

READ: Mark 12:29-31 – The command to "love your neighbor as yourself" is equally important as what other commandment?

13:11-14 – "This is all more urgent, (see vs. 8) for you know how late it is; time is running out. Wake up, for our salvation is nearer now than when we first believed. The night is almost gone; the day of salvation will soon be here. So remove your dark deeds like dirty clothes, and put on the shining armor of right living. Because we belong to the day, we must live decent lives for all to see. Don't participate in the darkness of wild parties and drunkenness, or in sexual promiscuity and immoral living, or in quarreling and jealousy. Instead, clothe yourself with the presence of the Lord Jesus Christ. And don't let yourself think about ways to indulge your evil desires."

Church of Christ—there is no time for napping!

God has called His people to live differently—to be light in an age where darkness reigns. To do so, we must *choose* to give Jesus Christ control of our life. As we obediently yield to His authority, the temptations of darkness will be defeated by His LIGHT.

As followers of Jesus, we are called to bring truth and light to those who are lost and deceived by darkness. This responsibility takes commitment and preparation, because the ruler of darkness hates truth and light and wars against it. But God has given us a powerhouse of spiritual armor that unleashes His LIGHT and sends darkness into hiding.

As we go forth, grounded in God's truth and wearing His righteousness, we are not only kept from wandering down dark paths, but have the power and wisdom to live in His LIGHT—sharing truth with those we meet along the way. (I John 1:7) And by having faith that is deeply rooted in Christ, we expose the lies of the enemy and can bring the hope of salvation to those who are trapped in the darkness.

Time is running out. Staying alert and being persistent in prayer—a vital part of our spiritual arsenal that will help us live as people of light—producing only what is good and right and true. (Eph. 5:8-9, 6:13-18)

CHALLENGE: "You are a chosen people. You are royal priests, a holy nation, God's very own possession. As a result, you can show others the love of God, for He called you out of the darkness into His wonderful light."

READ: I Thessalonians 5:1-4 – As children of light, what special event will not be a surprise to us?

READ: Proverbs 4:18-19 – What does this passage point out that should stir our compassion for those in darkness?

DAY 92

14:1-4 – "Accept other believers who are weak in faith, and don't argue with them about what they think is right or wrong. For instance, one person believes it's all right to eat anything. But another believer with a sensitive conscience will eat only vegetables. Those who feel free to eat anything must not look down on those who don't. And those who don't eat certain foods must not condemn those who do, for God has accepted them. Who are you to condemn someone else's servant? Their own master will judge whether they stand or fall. And with the Lord's help, they will stand and receive His approval."

God does the calling, preparing, and judging.

I've heard of young mothers who get very upset when they see another child walking at a year old and hers is still crawling. Or when she hears a friend's toddler speaking clearly and hers still can't make their 'R" or "L" sounds. These mothers soon learn that each child grows and develops at his own speed. It's the same within the church of Christ.

We all come from different backgrounds and experiences that influence how we live and grow in our faith. I know a man who has a problem with a certain type of music because he associates it with a dark time in his past. However, that same music reminds me of days that were filled with fun and were free of heavy responsibility. Our experiences were very different, therefore our view and conviction concerning the music is different.

Paul is telling his readers that because we all grow and learn differently, in love and for the sake of unity, we must not judge or set about trying to change one another—*that is God's job.*

Within the church of Rome were new converts whose past included idol worship. They steered away from anything associated with their old pagan experiences—like eating meat that had been sacrificed to idols. However, the believers who didn't have this experience in their past saw no problem with eating this meat. Paul tells his readers to be kind and not judge one another for their different convictions. He knew that as each one grew stronger in their knowledge of truth and deeper in their faith in Jesus Christ, the Spirit of God would help them grow in unity.

We each live and serve God at different levels of spiritual maturity and are accountable to Him for our walk of faith.

154

CHALLENGE: We need to realize that letting God be GOD has greater results than when we attempt to take over His job.

READ: I Corinthians 8:1-3 – Looking past the issue of eating food offered to idols, what truth does Paul point out that is clearly more vital to believers even today?

READ: John 5:22 and II Corinthians 5:10 – According to these verses, who is our judge and who gave Him the authority to judge?

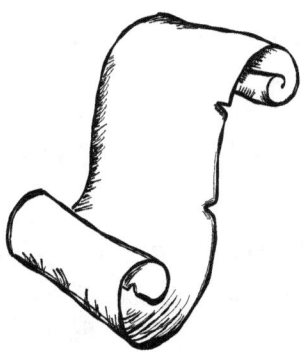

DAY 93

14:5-7 – "In the same way, some think one day is more holy than another day. While others think every day is alike. You should each be fully convinced that whichever day you choose is acceptable. Those who worship the Lord on a special day do it to honor Him. Those who eat any kind of food do so to honor the Lord, since they give thanks to God before eating. And those who refuse to eat certain foods also want to please the Lord and give thanks to God. For we don't live for ourselves or die for ourselves."

God will receive our honor and praise wherever and whenever our heart desires to worship Him.

If I was hiking in the mountains on a Thursday and the majesty of it all stirred me to honor its creator, would God reject my worship because it wasn't Sunday? Of course not. What if I went to church on Sunday and was mad at the world and feeling bitter toward my neighbor; would my heart and worship be acceptable to God just because it was Sunday? Again, of course not. God looks at the heart!

If our heart's desire is to honor God in what we do, He knows it—and it pleases Him. We cannot see or know the hearts of others. Therefore, we cannot judge them. Each of us has to discern for ourselves where *our heart is* and if we're honoring God in what we do. It is ultimately between us and God.

However, the Lord has given us guidelines in His word to help us grow in our spiritual life and to help us edify one another. He has told us not to neglect meeting together. (Heb. 10:25) He knows we need each other. We are told to be careful not to cause each other to stumble. (Rom. 14:21-22) We all grow at a different pace and we must not trample on each other. Being zealous for spiritual growth in others is honorable, but *it's God's job to work in hearts*. Our job is to love and edify one another.

Paul knew the church would be strong if each member's focus was on honoring God in all they did. This is true for our churches today.

CHALLENGE: We must let *God* work in hearts to bring us along to unity and spiritual maturity and not try to drive each other in directions *we* think need to be taken.

READ: I Samuel 16:7 and Psalm 33:15 – What do these verses tell you about your heart?

READ: Proverbs 4:23 and 27:19 – Why is our heart so important to God?

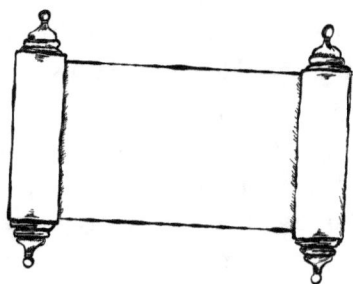

DAY 94

14:7-9 – "For we don't live for ourselves or die for ourselves. If we live, it's to honor the Lord. And if we die, it's to honor the Lord. So, whether we live or die, we belong to the Lord. Christ died and rose again for this very purpose—to be Lord both of the living and of the dead."

God paid a high price to be able to be our GOD.

Let's recap what we've learned so far. God created us, and because of our sin we were separated from Him. Out of His great love for us and to make it possible for us to be one with Him again, *He paid* our sin debt with the life of His own Son. Therefore, it's truth to say that we are not our own—we belong to God.

There are many who resent this truth. They see God as a controlling, bossy, glory-hungry taskmaster—wanting everything His way. They fail to acknowledge Him as their Creator—as GOD! We learned the fate of those with this attitude in chapter one of our study.

"Yes, they knew God, but they wouldn't worship Him as God or even give Him thanks. And they began to think up foolish ideas of what God was like. As a result, their minds became dark and confused." (Rom 1:21) How this kind of thinking must break God's heart!

As we study the Scriptures, we come to know the person and character of God, which leads us to this truth—that He is the only One worthy to be our God. We see that He is wise and holds the key to all wisdom and knowledge. (Rom. 16:27, Col. 2:3) That He is loving and kind, compassionate, patient, and faithful—and that He sincerely loves us. (Ps. 86:15) The Scriptures reveal His unchanging plans for mankind as a whole and His personal plan for each one of us as well. (Jer. 29:11-13, Micah 6:8) They speak of the freedom He offers us—freedom from sin and its consequences, freedom to make choices, and the freedom we gain from knowing and obeying His word. (John 8:31-32, I Cor. 6:12) We find that God is all powerful and that He has given us access to His power through the Holy Spirit. (Ps. 147:5, II Tim. 1:7)

Who has earned the right to hold our life in His hands? The One who gave us our life in the first place, then bought us back with the blood of His Son to secure our *eternal life*. Even now He is preparing a place for us to live with Him—and each other—for eternity. (John 14:1-3)

Choosing to make God the Lord of your life does not just honor Him; it is the key that unlocks the door to God's powerhouse. It allows His Spirit to accomplish in you those things that you cannot do on your own. (John 15:5)

CHALLENGE: We must make it our goal daily, to put our life in God's hands, allowing His perfect will to be accomplished in and through us.

READ: Isaiah 43:7 and I Corinthians 6:20 – Record the reasons mentioned in these verses for giving honor to God.

READ: Jeremiah 10:23 – Talk to God about this verse. Share your heart and thoughts with Him concerning the truth found here and let Him speak to you.

DAY 95

14:10-13 – "So why do you condemn another believer? Why do you look down on another believer? Remember, we will all stand before the judgment seat of God. For the Scriptures say, 'As surely as I live,' says the LORD, 'every knee will bend to me, and every tongue will confess and give praise to God.' Yes, each of us will give a personal account to God. So let's stop condemning each other. Decide instead to live in such a way that you will not cause another believer to stumble and fall."

One day we will ALL stand before God and acknowledge HIM AS GOD.

I've tried to imagine myself on that day. How will I feel? What will I do and say? Perhaps you've done the same. One thing I know for sure; I will not be standing. After looking into the Lord's eyes, how could I not fall on my knees at His feet? My Savior!!

The Scriptures say we will then give an account of ourselves. I'm not sure how God will do this, I just know that at the end I want to hear Him say, "Well done, thou good and faithful servant." (Matt. 25:21)

In today's passage Paul is using a quote from the prophet Isaiah in an attempt to stamp out a problem in the church that we still battle today—judging one another. "Why do you condemn another?", Paul asks. Is it not enough to be responsible for our own life?

God has not commanded us to judge one another. We are told instead to edify, build up, one another. (I Thess. 5:11)

The question then arises concerning the difference between judging and discerning—it's what we are supposed to do. Let's say it like this: Judging is determining what someone else's position or condition is or should be. Discerning is determining what MY OWN position or condition is or should be. If we spend our time and effort doing the one, we won't have time to do the other…and that goes both ways.

CHALLENGE: We must work hard at gaining understanding/discernment, and building each other up. Then let God be the judge. (Phil 1:9)

READ: James 4:10 – What is this verse saying?

READ: II Corinthians 5:10 – What will every human being do in their future?

READ: John 5:22 and Acts 10:42 – Who has been given authority to judge and who gave them the authority?

DAY 96

14:14-17 – "I know and am convinced on the authority of the LORD Jesus that no food, in and of itself, is wrong to eat. But if someone believes it is wrong, then for that person it is wrong. And if another believer is distressed by what you eat, you are not acting in love if you eat it. Don't let your eating ruin someone for whom Christ died. Then you will not be criticized for doing something you believe is good. For the Kingdom of God is not a matter of what we eat or drink, but of living a life of goodness and peace and joy in the Holy Spirit."

We are to be respectful to others when it comes to our personal freedoms.

Here again we see Paul's reminder to "edify, not crucify." Compassion and concern for others should always take precedence over our personal freedoms. There's a time and place for everything and we must choose wisely when it comes to this subject.

For example. We're having dinner at a restaurant with a friend who loves Coke but believes it's wrong for her to drink it because the caffeine causes her to be out of control with nervousness and stress and she can't be her best for the Lord. What do we do? Drink it in front of her—after all, it doesn't bother us—or order something else and have a Coke when we get home? Or, what if we're driving with a friend who is bothered by a certain type of music—believing it is offensive to God. Do we stick in a CD of this type of music and try to convince them it's okay, or put in something we can both enjoy and listen to the other music later?

These examples may seem silly to some, but for others, they may be very serious. It's not up to us to decide what the standard of right and wrong should be for others.

Some subjects are not directly addressed in the Scriptures. In these cases, we look for a Godly standard that IS addressed. The Scriptures don't speak about drinking soda pop. But they do say we are to give God our best and honor Him in everything we do—even with our body—which some may find difficult when it makes them nervous and stressed. (I Cor. 6:20)

The Kingdom of God is first about the Good News of Jesus Christ, hope for the lost, forgiveness for sin, and eternal life. *How* we are to live in His kingdom is determined by the Scriptures and the Spirit of God living in us. He will lead each of us along *as He sees fit*—never deviating from His Word. Our job is to follow and obey.

CHALLENGE: Goodness, peace, and joy are characteristics of the Kingdom of God. We must—as it's inhabitants—do all we can to help each other experience these virtues to the fullest.

READ: I Corinthians 8:9 and Galatians 5:13 – What do these verses say about personal freedom?

READ: I Corinthians 6:12 and I Peter 2:16 – What warnings are we given here concerning personal freedom?

163

DAY 97

14:18-23 – "If you serve Christ with this attitude, (see vs 17) you will please God, and others will approve of you, too. So then, let us aim for harmony in the church and try to build each other up. Don't tear apart the work of God over what you eat. Remember, all foods are acceptable, but it is wrong to eat something if it makes another person stumble. It is better not to eat meat or drink wine or do anything else if it might cause another believer to stumble. You may believe there's nothing wrong with what you are doing, but keep it between yourself and God. Blessed are those who don't feel guilty for doing something they have decided is right. But if you have doubts about whether or not you should eat something, you are sinning if you go ahead and do it. For you are not following your convictions. If you do anything you believe is not right, you are sinning."

As the Potter, it's God's job to form us—we are not responsible for forming each other.

Being considerate of each other's convictions must be a priority if there is to be unity and harmony within the body of Christ. Because we have *different* preferences, *different* experiences, and grow and learn in *different* ways and at a *different* pace, our personal convictions will vary. It is vital that we not criticize others when they see things differently and don't share our convictions—yet, at the same time, we must remain faithful to our own.

Only God knows each and every heart and where we are in our spiritual journey together. If we are convinced in our heart concerning a certain area or issue, we must—in obedience—respond accordingly. For we are accountable to God for doing things the way HE has personally instructed us in His word and by His Spirit. And we must allow others to do the same.

I have learned over the years that our convictions may change as we grow in our knowledge of God and His word. However, this can only be true in areas that are *not* specifically spelled out in the Scriptures or do not go against godly principles that *are* spelled out. For we know that God and His word never change.

We must show each other *grace* in the areas that God has allowed us freedom to choose. Trying to critique each other's convictions can get messy and we don't have the tools to do it correctly. This is God's job and it will be done in such a way that the *God of all grace* will get *ALL* the glory and praise for a harmonious and edifying outcome.

164

CHALLENGE: We must respect the convictions of others in the same way we want others to respect ours.

READ: Daniel 1:8 and Leviticus 11:41-44 – Daniel determined in his heart to follow the law God had given to his people. How can this encourage us when it comes to our personal convictions?

READ: I Corinthians 13:4-6 – How can these verses apply to today's study?

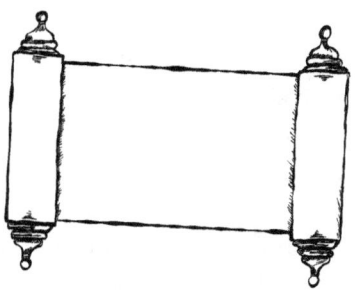

DAY 98

15:1-6 – "We who are strong must be considerate of those who are sensitive about things like this. We must not just please ourselves. We should help others do what is right and build them up in the Lord. For even Christ didn't live to please himself. As the Scriptures say, 'The insults of those who insult you, O God, have fallen on me.' Such things were written in the Scriptures long ago to teach us. And the Scriptures give us hope and encouragement as we wait patiently for God's promises to be fulfilled. May God, who gives this patience and encouragement, help you live in complete harmony with each other, as is fitting for followers of Christ Jesus. Then all of you can join together with one voice, giving praise and glory to God, the Father of our Lord Jesus Christ."

Throughout Scripture we see the words and phrases "one another," "each other," and "together." It is obvious that God sees unity and edification as foundational characteristics for a healthy church family.

The strong in faith need to be considerate of their weaker brethren, helping to build them up so they don't become discouraged.

It would be unfair for an experienced weightlifter to tell a beginner he had to be able to bench press two hundred and fifty pounds by the end of the week to qualify for the team. After a few attempts, the beginner may become discouraged and give up. But if the experienced one would come alongside the beginner to help him build up their strength, OVER TIME, he would be encouraged to keep going.

Paul is telling the strong in faith not to simply be content in their own strength. He says even Jesus got involved in the lives of others and it wasn't always comfortable. Those who are strong in faith must not become impatient with their weaker brethren or give up on them. They ought, instead, to come along side and patiently help them become stronger. It's all about "each other", "together" and "one another".

God tells us to build each other up, to encourage one another, to love and pray for each other, and *together* wait for His plan and promises to be fulfilled and for our eternal hope to become reality. We cannot do this if we choose not to be a participant. (see Eph. 6:18, I Thess.5:11)

To be able to watch a brother or sister in the Lord grow in their knowledge and faith is a privilege and joy. If we are sitting on the bench, we miss out. God wants us to be involved in the edification of His saints. He gives us everything we need to help one another grow to spiritual maturity and to experience harmony within the church. As His family and followers of Christ, we give Him glory and praise TOGETHER! He grows us so we can help grow each other.

CHALLENGE: We have to take our eyes off our self before we can focus on others.

READ: Colossians 1:9-11 – What was Paul's prayer for the saints in Colossae?

READ: Ecclesiastes 4:9-10 – Why are we not to be and "island"?

READ: Hebrews 10:23-25 – Why is it important to be "together"?

DAY 99

15:7-13 – "Therefore, accept each other just as Christ has accepted you so that God will be given glory. Remember that Christ came as a servant to the Jews to show that God is true to the promises He made to their ancestors. He also came so that the Gentiles might give glory to God for His mercies to them. That is what the psalmist meant when he wrote: 'For this, I will praise you among the Gentiles; I will sing praises to your name.' And in another place it is written, 'Rejoice with His people you Gentiles.' And yet again, 'Praise the Lord, all you Gentiles. Praise him, all you people of the earth.' And in another place Isaiah said, 'The heir to David's throne will come, and He will rule over the Gentiles. They will place their hope on Him.' I pray that God, the source of hope, will fill you completely with joy and peace because you trust in Him. Then you will overflow with confident hope through the power of the Holy Spirit."

The Gentiles were not God's second choice or His recalculated plan because Israel failed to do what they were supposed to do.

The Gentiles have always been included in God's plan for redeeming mankind. John 3:16 says God loved the world—all people—and gave up His Son so that "whosoever" believes in Him will have eternal life. And we learned in Romans 2:11 that God doesn't show favoritism. However, the Jews and Gentiles do have different roles in God's plan. He used Israel to reveal Himself to the rest of the world.

The Gentiles were introduced to God by seeing His mighty acts performed on behalf of the Jews. King Nebuchadnezzar saw God's power when He rescued the Hebrew men from the fiery furnace. When God saved Daniel from the lions, King Darius proclaimed throughout the world that Daniel's God is the "living God who will endure forever and His rule will never end." Kingdoms feared the God of Israel who fought for them against their enemies. All the people fell on their faces crying, "The Lord—He is God." when they watched fire from heaven consume Elijah's sacrifice. And the Roman soldiers were terrified at the crucifixion as God shook the earth, causing rocks to split and tombs to open—letting their captives free. They declared, "This man truly was the Son of God." (Dan. 3:29, Dan. 6:25-26, II Chron. 20:29, I Kings 18:38-39, Matt. 27:51-54)

When the Lord sent Paul to minister to the Gentiles, many were ready to hear. His prayer was that both Jews and Gentiles alike would be filled completely with joy and peace and that their hope would overflow because of their faith in God. Paul knew this would lead to mutual love and acceptance.

CHALLENGE: We must keep our eyes on the One we love and follow—accepting one another just as God has accepted us.

READ: Acts 22:21 – What did the Lord tell Paul?

READ: Acts 10:44-47 – What amazed the Jews and what is the bond that binds Jews and Gentiles together, making them one in Christ Jesus?

DAY 100

15:14-16 – "I am fully convinced, my dear brothers and sisters, that you are full of goodness. You know these things so well you can teach each other all about them. Even so, I have been bold enough to write about some of these points, knowing that all you need is this reminder. For by God's grace, I am a special messenger from Christ Jesus to you Gentiles. I bring you the Good News so that I might present you as an acceptable offering to God made holy by the Holy Spirit."

Paul was passionately committed to his ministry.

God had assigned Paul the mission of sharing the Good News with the Gentiles and he saw it as a great privilege. He whole-heartedly taught them what he had been taught and rejoiced as he watched them put their faith in Christ Jesus. But it didn't end there. They continued to grow in their knowledge of spiritual truth and were even able to teach each other. Even so, Paul's ministry did not *exclude* the Jews.

In Acts 9:15 Jesus said Paul was His chosen instrument to take His message to the Gentiles, to kings, *and* to the people of Israel. Paul's heart ached for his people as he diligently prayed for their salvation. God heard those prayers and many Jews became believers through his ministry. (Rom. 9:2-3, Rom. 10:1)

In Berea, Paul and Silas taught the Scriptures in the Jewish synagogue. As a result, many Jews and Gentiles believed. In Iconium, Paul and Barnabas preached in the Jewish synagogue with such power that a great number of both Jews and Gentiles became believers. In Antioch, as Paul and Barnabas left the synagogue, many Jews and devout converts to Judaism followed them, wanting to hear more.

Like Jesus, Paul suffered persecution at the hands of the Jews, but he also saw many put their faith in the risen Christ. He preached the Good News wherever he was sent and to all who were ready to listen. (Acts 17:10-12, 14:1, 13:42-43)

Paul saw every convert as a gift offering to God and another life to share in God's glorious inheritance.

CHALLENGE: As we serve the Lord, let us be open to being used in areas that we have not formerly been used, or with people who may be an exciting new experience and challenge for us.

READ: Matthew 4:18-22 – How prepared do you think these men were for their new ministry? Did it stop them?

READ: Exodus 3:11-12 – When God chose Moses for a special mission what was his response? What did God tell Moses concerning his response?

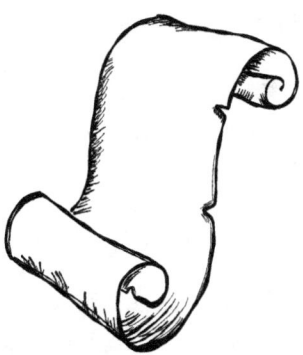

DAY 101

15:17-19 – "I have reason to be enthusiastic about all Christ Jesus has done through me in my service to God. Yet I dare not boast about anything except what Christ has done through me, bringing the Gentiles to God by my message and by the way I worked among them. They were convinced by the power of miraculous signs and wonders and by the power of God's Spirit. In this way, I have fully presented the Good News of Christ from Jerusalem all the way to Illyricum."

It's all about the plan, the message and the power of God.

Paul is taking no credit for the work being accomplished among the Gentiles. He sees himself as the voice, the hands, and the feet, chosen to be used to reach the Gentiles with the Good News of Jesus Christ.

It was the Father's *plan* from the beginning to redeem mankind, both Jew and Gentile. It was Christ's *message* of salvation through faith in Him alone. And it was the miraculous *power* of the Holy Spirit that convinced people the message was true.

Paul was a humble, willing servant, chosen by God, called by Christ Jesus, and enabled by the Holy Spirit to bring the Gentiles to God. He was enthusiastic about being a part of it all, but sincerely recognized that it was ALL accomplished by God—as he told the Ephesians, "so none of us can boast about it." He wrote to the Corinthians that he was given a thorn in his flesh to keep him from becoming proud. He knew it was the Lord's power at work. (Eph. 2:8-9, II Cor. 11:30, 12:7)

God's plan is to use disciples to make new disciples. He calls us to minister in different ways and in different places, and then enables us through the Spirit's power to use our God-given gifts in the building of His kingdom. (Acts 1:8)

The work is God's from the beginning to the end, and He is due ALL the glory.

CHALLENGE: As we serve God, let's remember who it is that enables us.

READ: Ephesians 3:6-7 – What do these verses tell us about Jewish and Gentile believers?

What does Paul say about his service to God?

READ: Acts 2:22, Mark 16:20, and Hebrews 2:3-4 – What do each of these verses tell us about the purpose of miracles?

172

15:20-22 – "My ambition has always been to preach the Good News where the name of Christ has never been heard, rather than where a church has already been started by someone else. I have been following the plan spoken of in the Scriptures, where it says, 'Those who have never been told about Him will see, and those who have never heard of Him will understand.' In fact, my visit to you has been delayed so long because I have been preaching in these places." (Isaiah 52:15)

I wonder what Paul thought about these writings from Isaiah before he saw the light.

After Paul's conversion and commissioning a lot of things must have finally come together for him. He had been taught the Scriptures and it's obvious that they were important to him. So far in our study of Romans we have seen him quote from Psalms, Deuteronomy, Isaiah, Leviticus, Hosea, Job, and II Chronicles. These passages must now have a whole new meaning for him. Now he sees the "nations/Gentiles" as people who need Christ— people who need to hear the Gospel. They are no longer considered outsiders. It is no longer Jew or Gentile—it is now those who follow Christ or those who still need to hear. (Acts 20:21) He must keep going—keep proclaiming the Good News of Jesus Christ where it had not yet been proclaimed.

It would have been an easier task to go in and plant where someone else had labored and perhaps suffered while breaking the ground. But Paul would not do that. He was determined to preach the truth wherever it had *not been heard*—wherever there was *a need to hear*. He knew there would be objections, he had experienced rejection and persecution in several places. Nevertheless, he was determined to go.

Nothing stopped him. He wrote letters from prison to encourage believers and to keep the Good News going forth. He went back and preached where he had previously been stoned. He boldly spoke truth before high councils and confronted hostile Jews with the truth. He saw each person and place as his mission field. He told the Corinthians he was compelled by God to preach the Good News and it would be terrible for him not to do it. (Acts 14:19-22,17, 22, 23, I Cor. 9:16)

For Paul, there was nothing more important than telling people the Good News of forgiveness and salvation through faith in Jesus Christ, and encouraging believers to grow in their knowledge of God. Toward the end of his life he told Timothy he had fought the good fight, finished the race, and had remained faithful. Now he was ready to hear, "Well done, my good and faithful servant." (II Tim. 4:7, Matt. 25:23)

CHALLENGE: Like Jesus, Paul often used Scripture to support his message. We can do the same.

*Go back through the chapters we've studied in Romans and find Paul's quotes from the Old Testament. Make note of how he uses each one.

DAY 103

15:23-24 – "Now I have finished my work in these regions, and after all these long years of waiting, I am eager to visit you. I am planning to go to Spain, and when I do, I will stop off in Rome. After I have enjoyed your fellowship for a little while, you can provide for my journey."

When Paul was writing this from Corinth around 57 AD, he had no idea what lay ahead.

Paul may have had an inkling of what to expect when he arrived in Rome because he had met Aquila and Priscilla, who had been living in Rome before their recent arrival in Corinth. In Acts 20:22-23 we read that the Holy Spirit had warned Paul to expect trouble in all the cities he visited. But he would have little knowledge of the details—like his future beating and arrest in Jerusalem, the shipwreck that would leave him and the rest of the passengers stranded on the island of Malta, the miracles that God would enable him to perform during their stay on the island, or that he would live under house arrest for the next two years once he reached Rome.

At the time of his writing, all this was *still ahead* of him. But by the time he ended his visit to Rome in 63 AD, *he could look back* on it all and see God at work.

He could see why God brought Aquila and Priscilla to Corinth when He did. They no doubt were able to give him information concerning Rome. They too, were tent makers, and together they provided for themselves working at their trade. They even opened their home to Paul so he had a place to stay. When he left Corinth, they went with him as far as Ephesus, where they stayed on for a while to minister. (Acts 18:1-3,18-19)

He could see how God used the shipwreck and subsequent stay on the island to win the favor of his captors, who treated him kindly and ultimately allowed him to have his own place in Rome. Even though he was under house arrest, he was able to have visitors and continue to teach concerning Jesus Christ and the kingdom of God—*and no one tried to stop him.* (Acts 28:30-31)

When he wrote to the Romans, he was *looking ahead* to his future visit. When he left Rome, he could *look back* and see how God had strategically worked out His plan.

God today is building a kingdom of believers for Himself—the foundation for His kingdom is Jesus Christ, His Son. He chose Paul and then

175

enabled him to do *His* kingdom work. We serve the same God who worked in and through Paul's life and He desires to use us as well. As we surrender to His call, He will work out the details of His plan for us—just like He did for Paul.

CHALLENGE: Looking back at what God *has done* can keep us looking ahead to see what He *will do*.

READ: Colossians 4:7-14 – Paul wrote to the Colossians while he was under house arrest in Rome. How can you tell Paul had a lot of liberty in Rome? Make a list of all the people who were ministering there *with* Paul.

15:25-29 – "Before I come, I must go to Jerusalem to take a gift to the believers there. For you see, the believers in Macedonia and Achaia have eagerly taken up an offering for the poor among the believers in Jerusalem. They were glad to do this because they feel they owe a real debt to them. Since the Gentiles received the spiritual blessings of the Good News from the believers in Jerusalem, they feel the least they can do in return is to help them financially. As soon as I have delivered this money and completed this good deed of theirs, I will come to see you on my way to Spain. And I am sure that when I come, Christ will richly bless our time together."

How grateful are you for your spiritual roots and heritage?

The Gentile believers in the region of Greece were grateful to their Jewish brethren for sharing the Good News of Jesus with them. When they heard about their suffering in Jerusalem, they took up a collection to help give them relief. Paul mentions this perhaps in an attempt to stir up the believers in Rome to do the same.

Bible scholars believe the church in Rome was started by Jewish converts who came from Jerusalem. If so, Paul may be reminding them of their spiritual heritage.

Looking back at my own family history I can see how God used famine, war, and sickness—as well as the desire for religious freedom and devotion to family—to build for me a Christian heritage. A thread of love for the Lord Jesus Christ wove its way through generation after generation, leading up to the day I became a child of God.

Like the believers in Macedonia and Achaia we can be grateful for God's sovereign plan to give us hope and a priceless inheritance kept in heaven by God. (Rom.15:4, I Pet. I:3-5)

CHALLENGE: Retrace the steps, places, people, and circumstances that God lovingly wove into your life that led to your salvation.

READ: Psalm 107:1-2 – What do these verses encourage us to do?

READ: II Timothy 1:5 and 2:1-2 – How was God at work in Timothy's life—past, present, and future?

DAY 105

15:30-33 – "Dear brothers and sisters, I urge you in the name of our Lord Jesus Christ to join in my struggle by praying to God for me. Do this because of your love for me, given to you by the Holy Spirit. Pray that I will be rescued from those in Judea who refuse to obey God. Pray also that the believers there will be willing to accept the donation I am taking to Jerusalem. Then, by the will of God, I will be able to come to you with a joyful heart, and we will be an encouragement to each other. And now may God, who gives us His peace, be with you all. Amen."

Christians need each other!

Paul is asking to be spiritually supported—held up before the throne of the Most High God—through the prayers of his brethren. He's trusting they will faithfully do this because of their love for him. It is a shared love, a gift from the Holy Spirit. He is very specific in his requests. He has struggles to contend with. Traveling in itself can be difficult, with scheduling, finding rooms and transportation…not to mention bandits and other unexpected adversaries.

He asks to be rescued from any and all who oppose the Way of Jesus Christ. He's been slandered and run out of Antioch, stoned in Lystra, and beaten and imprisoned in Philippi and Jerusalem during his last visit. He knows he must expect the same in the days ahead.

He asks them to pray that the gift he is taking to the destitute believers in Jerusalem will be accepted. The question is, why would they not receive a free gift when they are in such need? We must remember the long-standing animosity among the Jews and Gentiles. To accept a gift from the Gentiles may seem traitorous to the *new Jewish converts*. Also, it had been rumored that Paul was preaching against following the law—and he would be the delivery man. His concerns are real and understandable.

His ultimate goal is to visit the saints in Rome after a successful and productive ministry among the believers in Jerusalem. They would then rejoice together and be encouraged through their fellowship. He ends this portion by sharing his desire and prayer on their behalf—that they will find peace in the presence of God. Recognizing God's presence can still the heart and calm thoughts and fears.

CHALLENGE: Seek to follow the examples given in this passage: Pray for one another *specifically*.

Encourage one another through fellowship, and focus on God's presence to find peace.

READ: Philippians 4:6-7 – Paul wrote to the Philippians from house arrest in Rome. How do you think these verses can be a personal testimony for Paul when you consider today's passage, written about three years earlier?

READ: Psalm 46:10-11 – What results from *knowing* God is present?

DAY 106

16:1-2 – "I commend to you our sister Phoebe, who is a deacon in the church in Cenchrea. Welcome her in the Lord as one who is worthy of honor among God's people. Help her in whatever she needs, for she has been helpful to many, and especially to me."

How would *our* commendation read?

Phoebe was a member of the church in Cenchrea—a suburb of Corinth. She was entrusted with carrying Paul's letter to the believers in Rome. This is believed to be the case because it was common to give a commendation of the message bearer so they would be well received along with the message.

We're not told her marital status or her reason for traveling to Rome. Paul doesn't say she is "the wife of" or "the widow of." It is unlikely that he would send a single lady on such a mission unless she had family or servants to accompany her. Most Bible students believe she, or her family, had a business that took her to Rome.

The Greek text says she was a patron to many Christians, including Paul. She was likely prosperous because of the business and was able to support others financially as well as being a worker/servant in the church.

We can speculate about some of this because we know something of the culture. One thing we know for sure is that Paul had a high regard for Phoebe and trusted her with the letter that future scholars of Scripture would refer to as "Paul's masterpiece."

King Solomon writes in Proverbs 22:1, "Choose a good name/reputation over great riches; being held in high esteem is better than silver or gold." Phoebe's reputation won her a place of honor among her brethren and co-laborers for Christ, resulting in her name going down in biblical history.

Christians bear the name of Christ. We are His representatives in the world. Like Phoebe, we are to love, support, and serve *one another* so the kingdom of God will multiply. Jesus said, "Your love for one another will prove to the world that you are my disciples." (John 13:35)

Paul asks the believers in Rome to "help her in whatever she needs." She has helped others and now she may need some help. This is what brotherly love is all about—being there for others as we show the world that we are Jesus' disciples.

CHALLENGE: Representing the name of Jesus Christ is a responsibility we must take seriously in every walk of life.

READ: Acts 4:12-13 – Being with Jesus had marked the lives of Peter and John. In what way was this evidence and a testimony to the members of the council?

READ: John 13:34 – What example did Jesus set?

READ: Ephesians 5:1-2 – What must we do?

181

DAY 107

16:3-6 – "Give my greetings to Priscilla and Aquila, my co-workers in the ministry of Christ Jesus. In fact, they once risked their lives for me. I am thankful to them, and so are all the Gentile churches. Also give my greetings to the church that meets in their home. Greet my dear friend Epenetus. He was the first person from the province of Asia to become a follower of Christ. Give my greetings to Mary, who has worked so hard for your benefit."

Getting to know some of the members of the Roman congregation has fascinated me, and I trust it will you as well. For the most part, this information has come from Pastor John MacArthur, who gives credit to J.B. Lightfoot and William Barclay for their in-depth study of these dear brethren. As we look at these scholars let's see what we can learn from those who have gone before us.

Priscilla and Aquila. Banished from Rome by Claudius Caesar, they had moved to Corinth, where they met Paul. They were not only Paul's co-workers in the ministry of Christ Jesus, they had been co-workers in their tent-making business as well as his hosts, for they shared their home with him. They had been of great help to Paul and were dear to his heart. Now, after the death of Claudius, they were back in Rome and serving the believers there. It would not have been a surprise to Paul that they hosted church gatherings in their home, for he had been a recipient of their generous hospitality in Corinth.

While they worked side by side, cutting and stitching tents together, I imagine they discussed the church at Rome and their beloved brethren there. I can hear them telling Paul that Epenetus—the first Asian convert—was a member of their fellowship. It must have given him great encouragement to know Epenetus was being discipled by these dear friends. And then there's Mary. She was part of Priscilla and Aquila's support team—working hard to help them in the ministry.

In Acts 18:24-26 we're told of Priscilla and Aquila meeting Apollos. He was an eloquent speaker who knew the Scriptures well and taught the way of the Lord with accuracy. However, he had not been taught the doctrine of the Holy Spirit. Priscilla and Aquila took him under their wing and taught him this blessed truth. He then went out teaching *all* he had learned. This dear couple knew the Scriptures and the Gospel and were skilled at teaching it to others. I can imagine Priscilla sitting with a group of ladies around her kitchen table responding with Truth as they fired questions at her. And I can see Aquila, putting away his canvas and stakes as men gathered around him to hear about the resurrection of the Messiah. Yes…this couple was dear to Paul's heart.

CHALLENGE: We are all given spiritual gifts to be used to edify one another. These believers didn't waste theirs—they faithfully used what God had given them in service to Christ and their fellow believers. They are a great example for each of us.

READ: Acts18:18-19 – What information are we given here concerning Priscilla and Aquila?

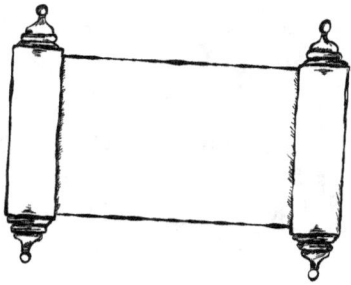

DAY 108

16:7 – "Greet Andronicus and Junia, my fellow Jews, who were in prison with me. They are highly respected among the apostles and became followers of Christ before I did."

The Interlinear Bible Greek translation – "Greet Andronicus and Junias, kinsmen of me and fellow prisoners with me, who are of note among the apostles, who also before me were in Christ."

It is truly a blessing when your family members share your love for the Lord Jesus.

Paul gave his greetings to Andronicus and Junias. I have read many commentaries on this verse and some believe they are husband and wife, while others say they are most likely both men. The name Junia/Junias can be either masculine or feminine—depending on how it is written. Like others, I believe they are perhaps brothers who are related to Paul. Notice in the Greek text he refers to them as "kinsmen." Perhaps they share the same human DNA as well as the same spiritual DNA! If this were the case, and because they were followers of Christ *before* Paul, think how it must have thrilled their hearts to hear of Paul's conversion. Their "kinsmen", who had been persecuting their fellow Christians, had given his life to Christ. What an amazing turn of events!

Somewhere along the time-line they actually shared a prison cell with Paul. I like to imagine them sitting together marveling over Paul's salvation story and praising God for His grace and mercy. What an encouragement they must have been to one another.

Paul says the other apostles respect them as well as he does. They were not "keep to themselves" believers. They are obviously on the front line, serving Christ, leading others in the Way, and being of service to the apostles. Whether they are related to Paul through physical birth or spiritual birth, he had a high regard for them.

If you have the opportunity of serving in your local church with family members, please be grateful for that privilege. But if God has you serving apart from your kinsmen, remember what Jesus said, "Anyone who does God's will is my brother and sister and mother." (Mark 3:35)

As Christians, in church we are never without family.

CHALLENGE: As long as we are all one family in Christ, let's bring delight to our Father by keeping our focus on Him as we fellowship and serve.

READ: Galatians 4:6 and I John 3:9-10 – What is the one thing all believers have in common and how is this made evident to the world?

READ: Acts 23:12-16 – Who was instrumental in saving Paul's life while he was in Jerusalem?

(You can read the whole story in Acts 23:12-30)

DAY 109

16:8-9 – "Greet Ampliatus, my dear friend in the Lord. Greet Urbanus, our co-worker in Christ, and my dear friend Stachys."
Galatians 3:28 – "There is no longer Jew or Gentile, slave or free, male and female. For you are all one in Christ Jesus."

In the family of God all members are equal. Romans 2:11 points out that God has no favorites. We are each saved by the grace of God, redeemed by the blood of Jesus, and temples of the Holy Spirit. I'm making this point because the next brother in the Lord that Paul greets may have been a slave.

In ancient times, Ampliatus was a common name among slaves. Paul calls Ampliatus his friend *in the Lord*. They had a mutual love and commitment to Christ that gave them this bond of friendship, reaching beyond the slave or free status.

Several years ago, I visited some catacombs in Rome. It was the resting place of many early Christians who had resided in Rome, and not all the tombs had inscriptions. But there was one particularly decorated tomb that was inscribed with the single name, "Ampliatus." We were told that it was possibly the tomb of Paul's friend.

The church in Rome is made up of people from many different places and from different walks of life—yet they are a close-knit group of Christians who love the Lord Jesus and with whom Paul had a history.

They are an example of the kind of unity and brotherly love that Paul preached and that Jesus prayed for on our behalf. (John 17:20-23)

CHALLENGE: It is said that there is strength in numbers. Let's keep our eyes on Christ and *together,* make His Good News known through our love and unity.

READ: Psalm 133:1 and II Chronicles 30:12 – The need for unity was not exclusive to the New Testament churches. How is the idea of unity seen in these Old Testament verses?

READ: I Corinthians 12:13 – Explain this verse in your own words.

READ: II Corinthians 6:1 – This verse *can be* both encouraging and convicting. It says we are God's partners—His co-workers. He shares His work of building His kingdom with us—trusting us to do our part. This is an amazing truth! Paul begs us not to accept this marvelous gift and *then just ignore it.* Working together *with* God and *for* God has eternal reward.

DAY 110

16:10 – "Greet Apelles, a good man whom Christ approves. And give Greetings to the believers from the household of Aristobulus."

Those who have experienced rejection in their life will find approval at the feet of Jesus.

Paul may not have personally known Apelles, but he knows of his strong faith in Christ. Apelles had at some point been put to the test and had come forth as gold. (Job 23:10) Paul says Apelles was "approved of by Christ" whose own Father declared, "This is my beloved Son, in whom I am well pleased." (Matt. 3:17) What a wonderful place to be—*in* Christ, who is *in* His Father and who is also *in* us. (John 14:20)

Having the life of Christ abiding in us and wearing His righteousness gives us a *permanent position* of approval by God. Recognizing this truth can free us from striving for acceptance by others and can shelter us from being hurt or disappointed when it is not freely offered.

The confidence that comes from having God's approval should never appear as pride, but it can certainly help us stand firm in our faith and lend boldness when it is needed.

As God's children, we are secure in our *position* of approval. However, God cannot and will not approve of sin. So, we must keep our *walk* worthy of our *position*. As Paul told Timothy, "Be an example to all believers in what you say, in the way you live, in your love, your faith, and your purity." (I Tim. 4:12)

CHALLENGE: Once we are in the *position* of being approved of by Christ, we ought to desire to have our *walk* live up to our position.

READ: II Timothy 2:15 – Is this verse speaking of our *position* of approval or of how our approval can be affected by our *walk?*

READ: I Peter 2:9 – Record how this verse can assure us that we are secure in our *position* in Christ Jesus.

188

READ: I Corinthians 10:13 – God has not given us His approval and then shaken us free to hold on to that approval alone. How can this verse encourage us in our *walk* with Jesus?

*Next time we will look at the household of Aristobulus.

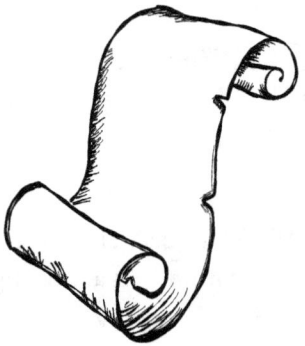

DAY 111

16:10b – 12 – "And give my greetings to the believers from the household of Aristobulus. Greet Herodion my fellow Jew. Greet the Lord's people from the household of Narcissus. Give my greetings to Tryphena and Tryphosa, the Lord's workers, and to dear Persis, who has worked so hard for the Lord."

Kids attending Sunday School, AWANA clubs, and youth groups have been the door to many parents coming to know Christ.

In today's passage Paul greets the Christians of the household of Aristobulus. He is believed to be the brother of Herod Agrippa I and the grandson of Herod the great. He also greets those who are believers in the household of Narcissus—very likely the former secretary to Claudius Caesar, a very wicked, devious man. Because Paul doesn't greet Aristobulus and Narcissus personally, we can assume they are non-believers, away from the house, or perhaps deceased. Whatever the case, the believers in these influential households have a unique opportunity to be witnesses for Jesus Christ.

Paul also greets a fellow believer named Herodion. The name itself connects him to the family of Herod; therefore, to Aristobulus. Paul refers to him as "kinsmen" as well. It's amazing to see how God did, and still does, use those within the house to reach others within the house.

Next to be greeted are Tryphena, Tryphosa, and Persis. These dear ladies labored much for the Lord. They are *involved* in the work of the ministry. This type of dedicated service is very much needed and appreciated in our churches today. Dads and moms need the Lord…kids need to be taught truth…lonely people need to be loved and cared for…sick people need compassion…and members need to be edified. There is a lot of work to be done!!

CHALLENGE: God has given each of us different gifts to be used within the church body. Let's use them to the fullest.

HISTORY LESSON:

READ: Matthew 2:16 – Herod the Great. What terrible act is he known to have committed according to this verse?

190

READ: Acts 12:1-3 – Herod Agrippa I. What actions of Herod Agrippa are listed here?

READ: Mark 6:14-16 – Herod Antipas. What does Herod admit to in this passage?

READ: Mark 6:20 – Luke 23:7-12. Reading the Mark passage gives one hope that Herod Antipas' heart may be open to God. What does Luke tell us?

READ: Joshua 24:15 – Believers taking a stand for Christ can result in many becoming His followers…in the home, in the church, and along the way.

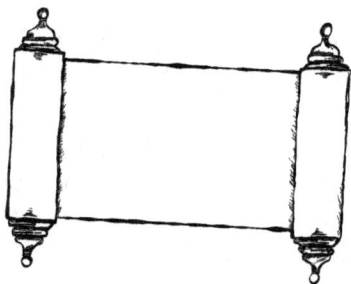

DAY 112

16:13 – "Greet Rufus, whom the Lord picked out to be His very own; and also, his dear mother, who has been a mother to me."

Being reminded of God's obvious handiwork in our life keeps our faith strong and our anticipation of future activity sharp—and we won't be let down.

Rufus is mentioned twice in the Bible. First by Paul, who greets him along with other believers in Rome, and later by Mark, who is in Rome and writing to the believers in the vicinity of Rome. (Mark 15:21)

When writing about the crucifixion, Mark says Simon from Cyrene was made to carry Jesus' cross; then he throws in that he was the father of Alexander and Rufus. It makes sense that Mark would point this out if Rufus was in their midst.

Paul tells us that Rufus was "picked out" by God to be His very own—as his father was "picked out" to carry the cross. Just imagine Rufus, following along behind Jesus and his father on the way to Mt. Calvary. Now, after many years, he is still following Jesus. Outstanding events can really impact one's life, and this one would be hard for a lad to forget.

God wants us to remember events that draw our focus to Him. After God dried up the Jordan River so the people of Israel could get across, Joshua set up twelve stones so that in the future, when the children asked what they meant, they could be told the wonderful story of God's mighty power. (Joshua 4:21-24) In Deuteronomy 4:9, Moses pleads with the people never to forget what they had seen—never to let the memories escape them as long as they lived. He knew that being reminded of God's presence and activity keeps us close to Him and our faith growing.

Obviously, Rufus and his mother were dear to Paul, but the husband/father is not mentioned. Perhaps he was deceased or away. Of one thing we can be sure, if Rufus was present on crucifixion day, and he watched his father carry the cross that would ultimately be raised up with the Son of God nailed to it, it would be something Rufus would never forget.

CHALLENGE: We ought to regularly look back and remember all the amazing times God showed us Himself and His mighty power.

READ: I Chronicles 16:12, Deuteronomy 8:2,18, 9:7 and II Timothy 2:8 – What are the people to remember?

DAY 113

16:14-16 – "Give my greetings to Asyncritus, Phlegon, Hermes, Patrobas, Hermas, and the brothers and sisters who meet with them. Give my greetings to Philologus, Julia, Nereus and his sister, and to Olympas and all the believers who meet with them. Greet each other in Christian love. All the churches of Christ send you their greetings."

Have you ever attended a different church while you were on vacation and felt totally at home with people who were complete strangers to you?

Obviously there had been communication between Paul and the church at Rome, and the information he received was thorough. Even though he had never visited them, he knew who the leaders were and how some of the members were related to each other. He then passed that information on to all the churches of Christ—such as those around Corinth who knew Paul was writing this letter.

The believers in Corinth had previously received letters from Paul while he was in Ephesus. Perhaps they remembered how encouraging it was to hear how the churches in other parts of the world were doing and how great it was to be greeted personally by their brethren in Christ—many of whom most likely had never met.

The spiritual connection between believers is supernatural. The indwelling Spirit of God gives believers spiritual camaraderie—affinity, togetherness, companionship, closeness, solidarity, and fellowship. The world cannot understand this kind of connection and devotion between people who may be total strangers to one another. But for those who feel alone and separated from the world around them, gaining a spiritual family through putting their faith in Christ would bring a huge change into their life. They would no longer be alone. As we said, you're never without family in church. They would begin to see a purpose for being alive in the world—others need the Lord. Who better to help them find Him?

A Christian is never alone. The Spirit of God living in us not only connects us to each other, but it also gives us a direct connection to our heavenly Father—who is always *with* us and at work *in* us.

CHALLENGE: Take every opportunity to encourage one another in your walk with Christ.

READ: John 1:12-13, Ephesians 2:19-21 and I John 3:1 – Why are Christians called "children of God" and why do those in the world not understand this truth?

READ: Ephesians 1:14 and 2:10 – As children of God, what do these verses say we are to do for Him?

16:17-20 – "And now I make one more appeal, my dear brothers and sisters. Watch out for people who cause divisions and upset people's faith by teaching things contrary to what you have been taught. Stay away from them. Such people are not serving Christ our Lord; they are serving their own personal interests. By smooth talk and glowing words they deceive innocent people. But everyone knows that you are obedient to the Lord. This makes me very happy. I want you to be wise in doing right and to stay innocent of any wrong. The God of peace will soon crush Satan under your feet. May the grace of our Lord Jesus be with you."

Unity is an element that is vitally needed in our churches if the kingdom of God is to continue to flourish.

Paul knows how important it is for truth to be taught and understood—and he does not underestimate the enemy. He warns his readers about people whose goal is to twist the truth; who selfishly take the spotlight and deceive those who are weak in their faith. He tells them, stay away from such people. He doesn't give instructions to try to correct or persuade them, he just says to "stay away" from them.

He has been encouraged by what he's heard concerning the saints in Rome and earnestly cares for their continued spiritual growth. His affection for this dear group of believers is sincere—they truly are his beloved brethren.

Paul sets a great example for us to follow. We too, must guard each other against false teachers who aim to divide us. We need to help those who are babes in Christ come to spiritual maturity by helping them grow in their knowledge of God and the Lord Jesus Christ. By the grace of God we are all one body, and we must take good care of each other. This kind of unity is what it takes for the world to see Christ in us, and for us to see spiritual maturity among the brethren. We owe it to each other—and are commanded by God to maintain a close relationship with Him—living in obedience to His word and allowing Him to do His work in us, in His church, and in the world around us.

CHALLENGE: I challenge each of you to do your part in encouraging unity within our church families.

READ: I Corinthians 12:26 – Give some examples of what is at the heart of this verse.

READ: I Corinthians 12:12-13 – What is it that binds believers together, making them one?

16:21-24 – "Timothy, my fellow worker, sends you his greetings, as do Lucius, Jason, and Sosipater, my fellow Jews. I, Tertius, the one writing this letter for Paul, send my greetings, too, as one of the Lord's followers. Gaius says hello to you. He is my host and also serves as host to the whole church. Erastus, the city treasurer, sends you his greetings, and so does our brother Quartus."

Like Paul, we are never expected to do the work of the ministry by ourselves. These verses introduce us to several of Paul's co-laborers, showing us the variety of workers God chooses to bring together to get the job done.

It's apparent that Paul wasn't alone much throughout his missionary travels. In his letters, he often mentions those who are with him as co-workers. He previously gave *his greetings* to many people in the Roman congregation. Now, several of his companions in Corinth send *their greetings* as well.

He first mentions Timothy—the young man whose Christian heritage was passed down to him by his grandmother, Lois, and his mother, Eunice. (II Tim. 1:5) He is often with Paul in his journeys, and was most likely the last person to receive a letter from Paul before he was executed. The next to give their greetings are Lucius, Jason, and Sosipater. We have some idea who these men are because they are mentioned elsewhere in the Scriptures.

Lucius was from Cyrene and is referred to as one of the prophets and teachers in the church at Antioch. (Acts 13:1)

Jason, from Thessalonica, once had his home attacked by a mob of hostile Jews who were searching for Paul and Silas. He was dragged before the city council, accused of treason against Caesar, and had to pay to get himself released. (Acts 17:5-9)

Sosipater is thought to be the same "Sopater" from Berea, who was traveling with Paul and is mentioned in Acts 20:4. He may have left Corinth with Paul as he traveled to Asia. Tertius, whose name means, "the Third", is writing the letter for Paul and takes this opportunity to say hello to the brethren as well.

Gauis of Derbe is next to send his greetings. He was often with Paul in his journeys and was once seized by a rioting mob in Ephesus for being a supporter of Jesus Christ. (Acts 19:23-29) It is also interesting to note that John's third letter is written to his friend Gaius. (III John 1:1)

Erastus, who we know was with Paul in both Ephesus and Corinth, was also a traveling companion to Timothy. According to Acts 19:22, Paul sent the two of them on ahead to minister in Macedonia. The final greeting comes from Quartus—"the Fourth"—who is a brother in the Lord.

Paul could not have done the work alone—and he didn't have to. God redeemed a host of men and women to assist Paul, and more recruits are still being added to His ranks every day.

CHALLENGE: Another history lesson reminds us we are not alone in the Kingdom calling. Remember, together we serve—together we plant—together we rejoice in what God is doing.

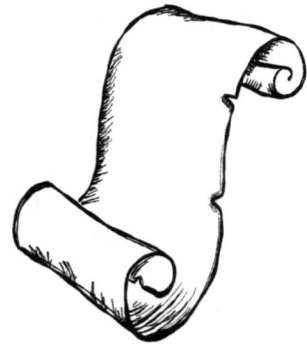

16:25-27 – "Now all glory to God, who is able to make you strong, just as my Good News says. This message about Jesus Christ has revealed His plan for you Gentiles, a plan kept secret from the beginning of time. But now as the prophets foretold and as the eternal God has commanded, this message is made known to all Gentiles everywhere, so that they too might believe and obey Him. All glory to the only wise God, through Jesus Christ, forever. Amen"

This letter, written by Paul, would now travel 780 miles in the possession of Phoebe—bathed in the prayers of its author.

The Good News of Jesus Christ was part of God's plan for mankind from the moment He breathed life into Adam. It was never an afterthought; it was never a response to mankind's activity. God had made Himself known to His creation from the very beginning. He established a relationship with Enoch, who walked with God. He spoke to Noah, who obeyed God. He made a promise to Abraham, who had faith in God, and there was Isaac, the fulfilled promise from God.

The nation of Israel was God's first chosen people. He used the Jews to show His love, faithfulness, and power to the Gentile world, who did not know Him—all the while knowing that one day they too would be invited into His family. The prophets of old had foretold this, but when that day came, the Jews would not accept it. Just as they refused to recognize that Jesus was the Messiah that the prophets had foreseen. But this did not stop God's plan. He sent His Son "so that everyone who believes in Him will not perish but have eternal life."—both Jew and Gentile. (see Hosea 2:23 and John 3:16)

Paul took no credit for the growing number of followers of Jesus. He gave all the glory to the only wise God, who sent His Son to be the Savior of the world. This is the message Paul preached—this is the Savior he served. He is remembered as one of the greatest apostles that ever lived. He was a Jew, who willingly, passionately and zealously shared the Good News of God's grace with the Gentile people.

When the letter was finished, I can imagine Paul wiping the sweat from his brow and kneeling down to thank God for all He had give him to say; praying that the truth in the letter would lead many to Christ and bring maturity to those who are in the household of faith.

CHALLENGE: May we continue to spread the message that God gave to Paul and was so dear to Paul's heart.